"This is a book that gives an accessible and practical vision of the circular economy, viewed through the eyes of two people who have played and continue to play a key role in its realisation."

Dame Ellen MacArthur, *Founder,*
Ellen MacArthur Foundation

"This book is a bold vision and a manual for a 21st century economy. A wake-up call."

Prof. Dr. Martin R. Stuchtey, *University of Innsbruck;*
Founder, Managing Partner, SYSTEMIQ

"A very inspiring and relevant book. We live in times of scepticism, doubt, negativism and populism. But only an agenda of hope takes us further. This is an important contribution to this agenda."

Prof. Dr. Jan Peter Balkenende, *Former Dutch Prime Minister*

"The products of today are the resources of tomorrow if we use them intelligently. This book shows us how."

Prof. Dr. Walter R. Stahel, *Leading expert on circular economy;*
Member of the Club of Rome; Founder -Director,
The Product-Life Institute, Geneva

D1680984

MATERIAL MATTERS

Our planet is a closed system with limited material resources, yet our current economic model is designed in a one-way direction from resource extraction to disposal, leading to resource depletion. This book proposes a new economic model, offering an alternative to this linear 'take-make-waste' economy.

Material Matters shows a way of creating a circular economy by using the unlimited resources we have: renewable energy, data and intelligence. It describes a system based on circular business models centered on selling performance rather than ownership, designing products and buildings as resource banks and equipping products with a 'material passport' to ensure their usability for future generations. Businesses thereby become custodians of materials, rather than consumers of materials and sellers of products. The book evokes the vision of a radically new economic model based on a compelling narrative, supported with cases that have been developed in conjunction with major companies, for example, convincing Philips to sell light instead of lamps, saving energy and materials by creating an entirely new business model, a case which has become iconic for the circular economy.

Material Matters is not a somber analysis of the state of the planet but an entirely and comprehensive agenda for change, offering perspectives for taking action for business and individual consumers alike.

THOMAS RAU is an architect, entrepreneur, innovator and recognized thought leader on sustainability and circular economy. His office RAU has been recognized for being at the forefront of producing innovative CO_2 neutral, energy positive and circular buildings as a norm. Thomas was elected as Dutch Architect of the Year 2013 and awarded with the ARC13 Oeuvre Award for his widespread contribution in both promoting and realizing sustainable architecture and bringing awareness of the circular economy through international delivered lectures, TV documentaries, TED talks and publications. In 2016, he was nominated for the Circular Economy leadership Award of the World Economic Forum. In 2021, he received the Circular Hero Award by the Dutch Ministry of Infrastructure.

SABINE OBERHUBER is an economist; together with Thomas Rau, she cofounded Turntoo, one of the first companies in the world focusing on the transition to a circular economy. Sabine is a renowned expert on circular economy; together with her team at Turntoo, she assists corporate clients and public institutions in the development and implementation of circular business models and management strategies and facilitates the transition to a circular economy. She studied economics at the Freie Wilhelms University in Münster (Germany) and received her Master of Management from the ESCP (EAP) European School of Management in Paris, Oxford and Berlin.

MATERIAL MATTERS

DEVELOPING BUSINESS FOR A CIRCULAR ECONOMY

Thomas Rau and Sabine Oberhuber

Routledge
Taylor & Francis Group

LONDON AND NEW YORK

Cover design: Scholz & Friends, edits by OneDesign

The translation was made by Roos van Hennekeler and edited by Dave Schmalz.

First published 2023
by Routledge
4 Park Square, Milton Park, Abingdon, Oxon OX14 4RN

and by Routledge
605 Third Avenue, New York, NY 10158

Routledge is an imprint of the Taylor & Francis Group, an informa business

© 2023 Thomas Rau and Sabine Oberhuber

British Library Cataloguing-in-Publication Data
A catalogue record for this book is available from the British Library

Library of Congress Cataloging-in-Publication Data
Names: Rau, Thomas (Architect), author. | Oberhuber, Sabine, author.
Title: Material matters: developing business for a circular economy /
Thomas Rau and Sabine Oberhuber.
Description: Abingdon, Oxon; New York, NY: Routledge, 2023. |
Includes bibliographical references. |
Identifiers: LCCN 2022031134 (print) | LCCN 2022031135 (ebook) |
ISBN 9781032193267 (hardback) | ISBN 9781032193274 (paperback) |
ISBN 9781003258674 (ebook)
Subjects: LCSH: Sustainable development. | Circular economy. |
Environmentalism—Economic aspects.
Classification: LCC HC79.E5 .R379 2023 (print) | LCC HC79.E5 (ebook) |
DDC 338.9/27—dc23/eng/20220818
LC record available at https://lccn.loc.gov/2022031134
LC ebook record available at https://lccn.loc.gov/2022031135

ISBN: 978-1-032-19326-7 (hbk)
ISBN: 978-1-032-19327-4 (pbk)
ISBN: 978-1-003-25867-4 (ebk)

DOI: 10.4324/9781003258674

Typeset in Minion Pro
by codeMantra

MIX
Paper from
responsible sources
FSC FSC® C013056
www.fsc.org

Printed and bound in Great Britain by
TJ Books Limited, Padstow, Cornwall

With gratitude to our children: Damian, Nathan and Laetitia
and our parents: Magdalene & Ulrich† and Stefanie & Wilhelm.

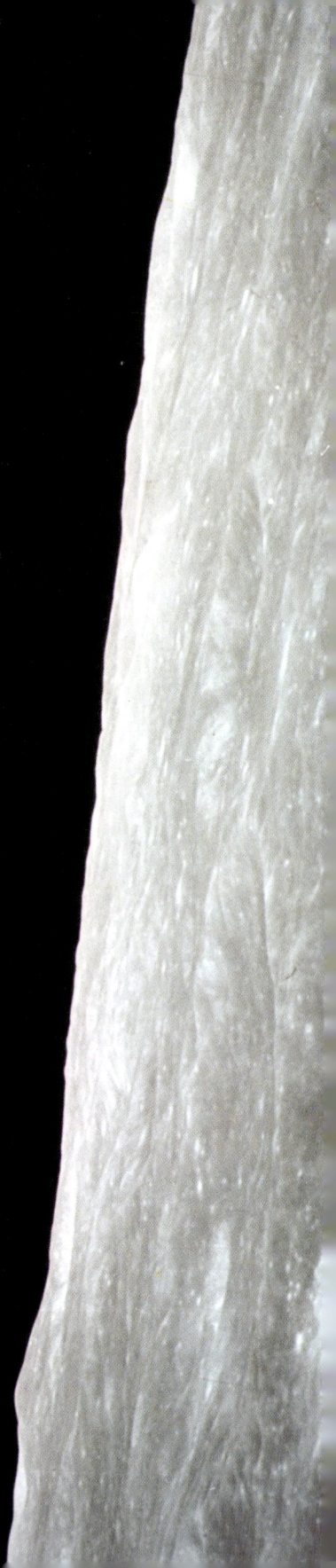

CONTENTS

CONTENTS

FOREWORD

Dame Ellen MacArthur

Sabine and Thomas have been part of my circular economy journey from the very early days; they were present in Davos in 2012 when we launched our first seminal report, 'Towards the Circular Economy,' which laid out the economic and business rationale for a circular economy for the very first time. Their first projects around this topic were ahead of their time and their ability to bring ideas to life demonstrates an outstanding understanding of the principles of the circular economy and how they can be applied in the real world. It is this practical application of the circular economy that grows increasingly crucial in the transition from linear to circular systems and makes this book such a timely and important one.

In this book, Sabine and Thomas not only discuss the rationale for changing the paradigm of material ownership and take-make-waste business models but they capture the essence of their many successful ideas and efforts to demonstrate that the circular economy can indeed be made into reality. A telling example of this is the idea that buildings should be seen as material banks, temporarily storing materials and conserving their value until they can be dismantled and reused elsewhere. Materials passports and registries can then be used to keep track of their identity and location so that they can eventually be recovered and continue to circulate within the economy. Reframing buildings and our approach to materials management in this way would bring multiple benefits such as eliminating waste and reducing resource extraction, which, in turn, serves to mitigate climate change and reduce biodiversity loss.

Sharing ideas such as these, and projects they have undertaken through RAU Architects and Turntoo, will undoubtedly inspire and help others, who are on circular economy journeys of their own, to do the same and in doing so will help to accelerate the transition from a linear to a circular economy. I would wager that if you should come across a library of circular economy case studies, you will more than likely find a Turntoo or RAU Architects example within.

This is a book that gives an accessible and practical vision of the circular economy, viewed through the eyes of two people who have played and continue to play a key role in its realization. I can only imagine that these pages will transport readers into Thomas and Sabine's thoughts and world. A world where materials don't just matter, but are understood to be precious and central to our lives, fully deserving of a universal declaration of rights such as the one shared at the end of this book.

Anyone who believes in indefinite growth in anything physical, on a physically finite planet, is either mad or an economist.

(KENNETH BOULDING)[1]

Introduction

DOI: 10.4324/9781003258674-1

We live in an age of vast and rapid change. Not a day passes without some of our established and trusted 'truths' falling apart. Every day we are faced with new realities; things we considered to be impossible until they happen – the reemergence of the cold war, whole economies being shut down due to a virus, long-established democracies coming under threat are just some of many examples we witnessed recently. At the same time extreme weather events breaking records year after year have nearly become the new normal. But is this really all that surprising, or did we simply miss the underlying causes? Have we been blind to the signs that were there all along?

For years, our global society has been presented with a plethora of interconnected, critical problems; ones that demanded our immediate attention, but also ones that we as a society far too long ignored and denied. For as long as we aren't directly confronted with the consequences of our actions and held accountable, we assume an apathetic attitude towards these problems. This shortsightedness is damaging. Only when urgent problems become so topical that they monopolize the day-to-day news, are we taking action, the tragic reality that by the time we act, it is usually too late for an adequate solution.

The corona virus is a strong warning sign, which showed us the interdependency and vulnerability of our globally connected economies and societies. A problem of even greater urgency is the environmental crisis, notably the change in our global climate. And although politics, business and society are slowly rising to the crisis. The action taken is still too little, too slow and hopefully not too late.

This crisis is caused by an economic system in which the values of the profit-and-loss account are the only "real" parameters for decision-making. Worse still, our culture is so imbued with one-sided economic thinking that this purely quantitative view of the world apparently justifies ignoring these crises.

The big global problems are also brought about by our linearly organized economic system, in which we extract, use and discard raw materials. Take, make and waste. This has led not only to a gigantic waste of raw materials but also to the loss of ecosystems and the climate crisis. Earth is a closed system, and our stay here is only temporary. Instead of behaving as responsible guests on this planet and conscientiously handling the resources that make our stay here possible, we have created a system that ignores the planetary boundaries[2] and endangers our very existence, and that of many other species as well.

Ever since the previous century, we have adopted an economic system, which is geared to continuous, exponential growth – our wealth depends on it. In order to maintain that system, products need to be consumed in ever greater quantities. Thus, we have allowed the products themselves to become a problem. Their technical life span is artificially shortened. Because of so-called 'innovation' we dispose of them before they are broken, and ever-changing fashion trends make us buy something new every season.

This system cannot be rectified through small adjustments. Instead, our economy needs to be reorganized in a fundamentally different way. Massive problems require massive solutions.

First of all, we must realize that ownership comes with accountability. Nowadays, all sorts of new possessions are forced upon us as consumers, for which we cannot carry any long-term responsibility. As soon as we want to dispose of a product for whatever reason we are unable to bear responsibility for all the resources and materials it contains – let alone reuse or recycle them. As consumers we simply lack the means to do so.

We can only solve this dilemma by changing our view on possession and ownership: by ensuring that we no longer have to own products in order to be able to use them.

We therefore have to steer toward a model in which producers remain responsible for their products, which means selling the functionality of a *product as a service* rather than the product itself. If ownership of products remains with the producer, *power* and *responsibility* for the materials are no longer separated, in this case producers have an interest to extend the life of their products and if handled in the right way, components and materials remain available for future products and automatically incentivize manufacturers to opt for better design and material choices. Only then can we see to it that we use materials without consuming and exhausting them.

In this model, valuable raw materials no longer end up as waste, but eternally keep circulating within our (economic) system. This requires new revenue models, and consistently keeping track of the location of materials, by means of material passports. After all, waste is in fact simply a collection of materials without an identity. But there is more to it: when we are actively aware of the fact that we use most products (and therefore raw materials) for a short time only, we also become aware of the fact that this – in the long run – applies to producers as well. We will therefore have to ask ourselves where right of ownership of the raw materials themselves should lie, or else the producer will eventually be overburdened too.

In our view therefore, throughout the whole production chain – from the original source to the user at the end of the process – we should redefine to what extent ownership is functional or indispensable. The consequence of that idea is that not only will products be sold as a service but materials will become a service as well. This way, a corresponding chain of value preservation is added to the existing chain of value creation, which will lead to a radical change in our global economic system; we call it the *Turntoo Model.*

However, in order to transform our economic system, we first need to be aware of the fact that the system is a reflection of our consciousness and our worldview. Although we have known since the sixteenth century that the Earth revolves around the sun, and that our planet is only one of many in an infinitely vast universe, we still behave as if man were the center of the cosmos. Everything is subordinated to our interests. This anthropocentric world-view provides the cultural foundation for the linear economic system described above. And it is this worldview that has brought us the crises we now face. To emerge from this crisis, it is important to not only change the rules of our economic system, but also, and crucially, we must change the soul of our economy and society.

Hence the title *Material Matters*. We must be aware of the fact that materials *do* matter, and that linked to this conversation are plenty of other interconnected, critical issues – *material matters* – that we urgently have to act upon, matters, *which are* material to our existence. After all, we are simply guests on this Earth.

For us, this knowledge triggered the establishment of RAU Architects in 1992. For decades now RAU is seen as one of the pioneers in sustainable architecture, constantly challenging the status quo of sustainable design and construction. Gradually, however, we saw that the questions we encountered lacked a certain dimension. The preservation of a habitable Earth requires more than just energy producing, healthy and durable buildings. That is why, in 2010, we started "Turntoo": the first organization in the Netherlands to focus on facilitating the transition toward a circular economy, and the development of business models which can ensure that valuable raw materials are no longer wasted, models we pioneered with major corporations such as Philips and Bosch. And because we believe that just like the limited surface of the earth is charted in a land registry, we need to register the limited material supplies of our planet in a material registry, we initiated "Madaster," the cadastre for material in 2017, a digital online platform, which generates and stores material passports for buildings and which is currently operating in eight countries. During the course of the last decade, we developed our concept, recognizing that the circular economy is indeed an important step, but that eventually further steps are required for a fundamental, complete transformation of the existing system. *Material Matters* outlines a new perspective for this transformation.

It is encouraging to see that ideas for a large-scale transformation of our economic system are receiving increased social attention. Many governments, public bodies and people in trades and industries are starting to awaken to the urgency of it. But, of course, this major movement has its front runners: people who for decades have championed such a transformation. Many of them we have had the privilege to meet personally on this journey, some of them have become valued friends, and we highly appreciate their work. Furthermore, this book does not presume to give the only and complete solution with regard to this major transformation. It is an attempt to add our own insights and experiences to this vital discussion, based on our practical experience as entrepreneurs.

What connects us all can be summarized in a quote attributed to Victor Hugo:

> There is nothing more powerful than an idea whose time has come.

NOTES

1 Boulding, K. (1973). Anyone who believes in indefinite growth in anything physical, on a physically finite planet, is either mad or an economist. Statement made at: U.S. Congress, Energy Reorganization Act of 1973: Hearings, Ninety-third Congress, First Session, on H.R. 11510, U.S. Government Printing Office, p. 248. https://www.govinfo.gov/app/details/CHRG-93hhrg25108O

2 Rockström, J., Steffen, W., Noone, K., et al. (2009). "A safe operating space for humanity." *Nature*, Vol. 461, pp. 472–475. https://doi.org/10.1038/461472a; "The Nine Planetary Boundaries." *The Nine Planetary Boundaries – Stockholm Resilience Centre*. The Stockholm Reslience Institute. https://www.stockholmresilience.org/research/planetary-boundaries/the-nine-planetary-boundaries.html

The key to economic prosperity is the organized creation of dissatisfaction.

(CHARLES F. KETTERING)[1]

CHAPTER ONE

The product-as-problem

We need a new smartphone every two years, our printer fails after a fixed amount of copies and yesterday's new shoes embarrass us today. Has this always been the case? How did dissatisfaction become the driving force of our economy?

DOI: 10.4324/9781003258674-2

In June 2011, about 500 people got together for a typical birthday party. They sang songs, they proposed a toast and they had cake as well as ice creams. The day ended with the recital of a solemn poem, written especially for the occasion: reaching the impressive age of 110. The center of all this attention? A light bulb.

The now-famous lamp started its life in the fire station of a small American town called Livermore, in 1901. It has been burning ever since, even surviving two relocations and several earthquakes. In 1976, it was included in the Guinness Book of Records as the oldest, still-burning light bulb in the world. At the light bulb's centennial in 2001, even President George W. Bush sent his congratulations, declaring the bulb "an enduring symbol of the American spirit of invention." Since then, the bulb has been under constant observation; for 24 hours a day, a webcam registers its every moment. It has its own website and dedicated custodians taking care of its well-being.

But while the "Centennial Lightbulb"[2] has been burning for over a million hours – a moment which was commemorated in 2015 with yet another celebration – the webcam that observes it had to be replaced three times already since its installation in 2001. Buy a comparable incandescent light bulb in the store today – roughly 120 years later – and it will only illuminate your kitchen for about 1,000 hours, before it burns out.

That raises a question: why don't all products last as long as the light bulb from 1901? How is it possible, that, in spite of our ever-increasing knowledge and technical skill, the average life span of a product has massively decreased, rather than increased? How did we get so used to throwing things away?

AND THERE WAS LIGHT

In 1879, the invention of the light bulb marked the ending of human dependency on candles and oil-lamps. Thomas Alva Edison is often credited for inventing the light bulb, but to call him the "inventor" is actually incorrect; the first "light bulb" (albeit *avant la lettre*) was invented as early as 1800, before Edison was even born.

He was, however, the first to perfect the procedure and start production. Edison, founder of the General Electric Company (GEC), was an astute businessman from New York who made a large part of his fortune buying and patenting inventions. When he shared the miracle that was electric light with the public, he famously proclaimed: "We're going to make electric light so cheap that only the rich will burn candles."

Edison's product was a direct solution to a problem anyone can relate to: darkness falls every night, candles and oil-lamps burn up quickly, not to mention their associated health and safety issues. Unsurprisingly, the GEC light bulb automatically generated prodigious demand and its success attracted more manufacturers to focus on the lucrative electric-light market. Economic competition between manufacturers caused the quality of light bulbs to increase rapidly: while the 1881 design could burn for about 1,500 hours, the 1924 design would already last about twice as long.

This started to worry producers. What if this trend would persist? Inevitably, they would reach a point at which new light bulbs would rarely be needed. Then what? This is how the light bulb illuminated the problem that lies at the heart of this business model: solve a problem too well and you risk making yourself redundant. How to keep your company from going bankrupt, when you have caused your own market to be saturated? No solution to that problem was available yet.

In his famous 1964 book *One-dimensional man,*[3] German philosopher Herbert Marcuse wrote that progress is not a neutral term: it moves toward specific ends and these ends are defined by the possibilities to improve the human condition. "Advanced industrial society is approaching the stage where continued progress would demand the radical subversion of the prevailing direction and organization of progress."

Marcuse's words point to the fact that technological progress can lead societies into a situation in which, in order to make sure that a society's wider idea of "progress" (i.e. progress outside of the technical dimension) determines the direction of its technological progress instead of the other way around, it needs to rethink certain forms of organization – such as business models.

Often these forms of organization have been working perfectly for years, sometimes even centuries. If this reorganization fails to happen, technological progress can end up causing enormous social problems – problems that will eventually spill over into the technological dimension, too.

Think about the recent discussion on artificial intelligence and automation as applied in production processes that traditionally rely on human labor: a token of progress if ever there was one. In a system in which human beings rely fully on the sale of labor for their livelihood, however, this token of progress (potentially) causes an enormous social disaster. And what happens when a significant share of the population loses their purchasing power? At some point, the motors of production, too, will grind to a halt. The incentive for technological development will die with them.

At this crossing, two different paths are available: one way is by curbing technological advancement, the other by redesigning the organization of progress. The way the light bulb manufacturers chose to solve their dilemma marks a turning point in economic history.

1,000-HOUR LIFE COMMITTEE

In response to the dilemma described above, a group of the most notable light bulb manufacturers (including General Electric as well as the German company Osram, the French Compagnie des Lampes and the Dutch Philips Company) established a secret cartel, which was meant to put an end to their problems. This cartel, founded on December 23, 1924, in Geneva, carved up the worldwide light bulb market, making it the first cartel in history with a truly global reach. From that moment on, as decided by the so-called "Phoebus cartel" (named after the Greek god of the sun: Phoebus Apollo) the

durability of a light bulb would have to be limited to a 1,000 hours. A special committee – "The 1000-hour Life Committee" – would make sure that companies all over the world would comply with this agreement. All light bulbs were tested in laboratories; if the amount of hours surpassed the 1,000-hour limit, companies could count on significant fines.[4,5]

In a paper published by Philips in 1928, the economic benefit of the cartel is clearly quantified:

> from a commercial point of view, it is of great importance to exceed the burning time of one thousand hours as little as possible, since every ten hours of additional burning time represents a loss of the global contingent of about one percent. If one is careful in the production, it is technically possible to reach an average lifespan of a thousand hours exactly.[6]

In his 2014 book *Geplanter Verschleiß* (*Planned Obsolescence*), the German professor of political economy Christian Kreiß writes that if we assume that the Phoebus cartel successfully reduced the average life span of a light bulb by about 1,000–1,500 hours, it follows that about 400–600 million light bulbs have been produced additionally (and thus unnecessarily) every year since 1925. Kreiß's calculation does not take into account global growth, however, which, of course, has been significant since then. Had he taken global growth into account, the number would have been a staggering multiple of his original estimate.

Public mention of the cartel was first made in Thomas Pynchon's 1973 novel *Gravity's Rainbow*,[7] which includes a whole chapter about a light bulb called "Byron the Bulb," who finds himself in the crosshairs of Phoebus: a wicked light bulb cartel controlling the life span of every bulb in the world. Since Pynchon was known for mixing facts with fiction, however, most people took the Phoebus cartel to be a product of his imagination. The existence of the Phoebus cartel was mentioned publicly for the first time in 1992, through an article in the German newspaper *Die Zeit*, in the middle of a fierce dispute over the sale of the East-German light bulb manufacturer *Narda*, which, in DDR times, had produced light bulbs with a burning time of 2,500 hours.

The evidence for the cartel's existence, which officially called itself the *International Electrical Association*, was discovered only as recently as 2010, when the original founding documents were discovered in Berlin's city archives, along with diagrams that showed the decrease of the average light bulb's life span between 1926 and 1934.

At the aforementioned cross-road, the light bulb manufacturers had chosen the path to curb technical progress, even to reverse it. The light bulb, once the symbol of technological advancement, was thus successfully turned into an inferior product and a new business model had been invented in the process: "planned obsolescence."

During the Great Depression, planned obsolescence was even openly discussed as a suitable strategy to boost economic growth. In 1932, a real estate broker called Bernard London published a paper called "Ending the Great Depression through Planned Obsolescence."[8] In this paper, London proposed that

> government (should) assign a lease of life to shoes and homes and machines, to all products of manufacture, mining and agriculture, when they are first created, and they would be sold and used within the term of their existence definitely known by the consumer. After the allotted time had expired, these things would be legally "dead" and would be controlled by the duly appointed governmental agency and destroyed if there is widespread unemployment.

He further proposed "that when a person continues to possess and use old clothing, automobiles and buildings, after they have passed their obsolescence date, as determined at the time they were created, he should be taxed for such continued use of what is legally "dead". " London was convinced that this model would result in creating demand and stimulating the repressed economy. Understandably, London's idea failed to gain traction – but his words did not go unnoticed.

It was Brooks Stevens, one of the most influential twentieth-century designers, who in 1954 gave planned obsolesce a definition, which would inspire designers and marketers alike: "instilling in the buyer the desire to own something a little newer, a little better, a little sooner than is necessary."[9] The idea has been applied by manufacturers all over the world: planned obsolescence has become a viable means of sustaining consistent consumption and profits.

NEW EQUALS *NOT BROKEN YET*

We have become used to the fact that it never takes products very long to stop functioning properly. The washing machine's Achilles' heel is either its pump, its PCB or its bearing; as a rule, one of these things breaks down after a few years, or after some X number of washing cycles. Cars are built so that it always takes a predetermined number of miles for the exhaust pipe, the gearbox and the engine to require replacement. Most printers contain clever chips that count the number of pages produced by the printer, so that after a specified number of copies it "knows" that it is supposed to stop working. Only insiders know how to press the reset button, after which the machine will function again. Instead of digital manipulation, simple mechanical tricks can also be used to shorten product life. A gearwheel made of plastic will inevitably wear out much faster when combined with one made of metal.

This is not only true for printers, the same mechanism applies to dishwashers and coffee machines. If products and appliances are reparable at all, the costs of these planned maintenance services, meanwhile, often add up to about 150% of purchase price – and the warranty period offers little consolation: it simply exactly covers the meticulously planned life span of the product. In some cases, spare parts simply are not even available. Trade associations typically do establish codes of practice including recommended periods for storing spare parts for the products they sell – but in some cases, these periods, incomprehensibly, are shorter than the average life span of the product. UK trade organization AMDEA (the Association of Manufacturers Domestic Electrical Appliances) recommends to its members that they keep spare parts for freezers and refrigerators for eight years, for instance, even though these kinds of appliances tend to last for 10–12 years.[10] The interminable waiting time that characterizes the average repair service functions as another incentive to throw the "old" one out and buy a new product instead. The market price of these replacement parts is usually negligible: it's the labor that makes these services so costly. In spite of all our technological knowledge, products are seldom designed in ways that make repairing them easy.

Many products, moreover, are so low in quality that repairing them simply isn't financially viable. The argument for low quality production is that products should be accessible to consumers on a smaller budget. Which might seem a valid argument if the cost savings of the parts, which are made to break anyway, are often just a tiny fraction of what the repair job costs. For example, a study carried out by the University of Pforzheim in Germany found that the material costs saved in the manufacture of certain part of a milk frother known to cause an error was in the range of 0.33%, which is almost nothing.[11] In addition, products which are made to break pose an even greater problem for consumers with a small budget.

To offer another example: *Halte à l'Obsolescence Programmée*, a French organization against planned obsolescence, conducted a study into women's consumption of tights. It found that on average women buy about 10–11 new pairs each season: not because they get bored with the ones they have, but because they cannot wear the ones they have anymore due to breakage.[12] This too is by no means inevitable, or a way to make tights accessible to consumers on a smaller budget: manufacturers have been playing with chemicals to make their nylon less durable. When the nylon stockings were first introduced in the 1940s, they became hugely successful not in the last place because they were marketed for their longevity – their robustness became legendary by an advertisement movie in which the stockings were used as a towing rope. But only a few years later, manufacturer DuPont forced its researchers to weaken their nylon, as their tights were lasting so long that they damaged the market.[13]

There was a time when products represented real solutions. However, these solutions have slowly but steadily turned into organized problems:

designed to fail. Our technical insights are not applied to optimize products, but to create defects or needs intentionally. The Swiss Consumer Protection Foundation differentiates between the following three types of defect: built-in counters, hidden weak spots (undersized components, weak points in the construction) and the use of unsuitable or cheap materials, such as using plastic instead of metal. The latter type is often used to create a kind of psychological effect, where non-vital parts of, for instance, a car are made of plastic so that they systematically break over time, leading the owner to mistrust the vehicle. According to a study on built-in obsolescence by the German Oeko Institute, the share of large household appliances that had to be replaced within the first five years grew from 7% of total replacements in 2004 to 13% in 2013.[14]

And according to Eurostat numbers dating from 2019, over 20 kg of electrical and electronic products are put on the market on average per person in the EU each year, including large household appliances such as washing machines and refrigerators, as well as electronics and gadgets such as computers, TVs and mobile phones.[15]

Designers and engineers do not determine the life span of an appliance or product; managers do. Craftsmanship and reliability are important only inasmuch as they relate to maximizing profit, with little or no regard for consumers or the environment. Manufacturers have thus successfully passed on their business problem to consumers, who perpetuate the problem by "solving" it with the purchase of a shiny new organized problem: the very heart of this business model.

NEW EQUALS *NOT QUITE OLD YET*

Unfortunately, technical manipulation is just one way of manufacturing organized problems. A more subtle form of planned obsolescence relates to the speed with which small, non-revolutionary innovations succeed each other on the market. Even though in this case the product won't stop "working" in the technical sense of the word, its value in relation to its larger context will decrease just as quickly. Not technical, but "functional" manipulation does the job here; designed to be outdated.

Nowadays, the predicate "new" usually doesn't refer to anything genuinely life-changing. Not in the way that cars provided us with unprecedented freedom, or in the way that the invention of the washing machine and refrigerator almost single-handedly allowed women to enter the labor market: by reducing the time needed for household chores from 58 hours a week in 1900 to 18 hours in 1975.[16] And what about innovational leaps like the invention of penicillin, anti-conception, the steam engine or the telephone?

Outside of information technology, innovation hasn't changed our day-to-day lives much in recent decades. Houses, appliances and cars look much like they did a generation ago, as journalist Greg Ip pointed out in a 2016 article in the *Wall Street Journal*.[17] Airplanes fly no faster than they did in the 1960s. None of the 20 most-prescribed drugs in the US came to the market in the past decade. We may feel like we live in the golden age of innovation (and the hyperbolic lexicon of the advertising business gladly encourages this image) but the reasons for that may have more to do with our focus than our actual daily reality.

Nowadays, when used in the context of consumer products, the word "innovation" usually refers to subtle changes in the design, meant to make last year's product appear hopelessly antiquated. Companies manipulate the expiration dates of their products by seducing consumers with minor product changes, that are nonetheless heavily marketed as innovative and life-changing.

Henry Ford is famous for revolutionizing the automobile market by being the first to standardize cars – famously employing the lines "You can have the Ford T in any color, as long as it is black." His contemporary and rival Alfred Sloan, long-time president of General Motors however, revolutionized the market by doing the exact opposite: playing into his clients' individual desires and creating the first marketing department – incorporating functional manipulation into his sales strategy. In his autobiography, Sloan recalls: "The changes in the new model had to be so new and so attractive that they would stimulate demand, and a certain amount of dissatisfaction with the models of the forerunners."[18]

The recipe has been copied by almost any sector to spur the sale of goods and the speed with which this happens has been increasing exponentially over the past decades: by 2012, more than 60% of televisions that were replaced with new televisions were still functioning perfectly.[19] By 2019, a survey carried out by a US consulting firm found that 84% of respondents had now replaced traditional television altogether – in favor of online streaming services. 62% said traditional television had become irrelevant.[20]

Smartphones are another example. Telecommunication companies design their phone plans to include strong incentives to replace your phone for a newer model after only a year or two. But the newest smartphone is (at best) slightly more advanced than its predecessor. Usually, the screen will be a bit bigger and sharper, the camera will take slightly better pictures and the consumer will receive one or two nice gimmicks, such as the fingerprint scanner or the ability to take a panorama photo. Not exactly life-changing innovations. Still, on average, consumers replace their mobile phone every one and a half years. Between 2009, when the first smartphone was released, and 2017, the staggering number of 8.2 billion smartphones has been sold, according to research company Gartner – of which 1.5 billion in 2017 alone.[21] Since then, the smartphone penetration rate has kept steadily rising. In 2018, 38% of the world's population owned a smartphone device. By 2020, this had risen to 46.5%. According to Gartner, this number will have grown by another 11% by the end of 2021.[22] In order to manufacture all those phones, more than 15,000 tons of copper, 350 tons of silver, 30 tons of gold and 14 tons of palladium are extracted from the earth every year.[23] Recycling rates, however, for electronic waste remain at a meager 20% globally, according to the EPA.[24]

To make matters worse, the value of hardware products usually depends on the device's compatibility with all sorts of accessories: a certain charger, earphones or specific software which is crucial to downloading the latest app. These accessories are usually not only made to break even more quickly than the phone itself, they also often put consumers in a fix, because while their device might still be "working" perfectly in a technical sense, due to a lack of compatibility, users find themselves unable to use the device for what is intended for. After all, staying up to date with the rest of the world is what most modern technology is all about. Consumers thus still find themselves compelled to buy a new device, regardless of whether or not their current one is broken.

The engineers at the big tech companies, with all their technological expertise, are certainly able to design a game console or a smartphone that can be upgraded with new features easily. But if they did, who would still buy a new one every other year?

NEW MEANS *NOT QUITE UNFASHIONABLE YET*

Finally, there is a third way to encourage consumers to buy new stuff. It was "invented" in the United States in the 1920s, after which it rapidly conquered the rest of the western world. The main character in this story is a man who has played a decisive role in recent world history, although his name remains largely unknown by the public: Edward Bernays. He was Sigmund Freud's nephew, and the first person to see (or at least put to use) the potential commercial value involved in his uncles' revolutionary understanding of the human psyche. Freud claimed that, (contrary to our experience) our actions and decisions are led mostly by subconscious desires rather than our ability to reason. This idea, first applied to the sale of goods by Bernays, formed the foundation for the advertising business we know today: *designed to go out of fashion or designed to become uncool.*

A famous example of the way Bernays first turned his uncle's idea into a sales strategy was described by filmmaker Adam Curtis in the BBC documentary *The Century of the Self.*[25] It concerns the way Bernays (successfully) convinced US women to start smoking. At the time of the 1920s, a smoking woman was considered vulgar. Dutch painters in the seventeenth century had used cigarettes as a symbol for social deviance and foolishness, and by the nineteenth century, cigarettes had become known as props for 'fallen women' and prostitutes. Naturally, this stigma – which still stuck to cigarettes in the 1920s – displeased the tobacco industry since it pretty much cut the number of potential buyers of cigarettes in half. They sought the help of Mr. Bernays: the first PR manager ever (not in the least because he invented the term himself).

Bernays hatched a plan. During the annual Easter Parade in New York City, a group of attractive young actresses would suddenly come to a halt and take out packs of cigarettes from under their skirts, after which they would all light one. In the meantime, Bernays would have spread the rumor that the girls were a group of suffragettes, protesting by smoking 'Torches of Freedom' against the suppression of women. His plan was executed and showered with attention by the press, just as Bernays had intended. The sales of cigarettes to women increased immediately and significantly. From that moment on, cigarettes were seen as a symbol for female independence.

As the establishment of the Phoebus Cartel marked the beginning of technical manipulation, so the Easter Parade marked the beginning of a new type of advertising (and relating to) products: linking tangible, purchasable products to subconscious desires, feelings of identity, cultural associations and symbols of status. As Paul Mazur, a Wall Street banker, suggested in 1927:

> We must shift America from a needs, to a desires culture. People must be trained to desire, to want new things even before the old has been entirely consumed. We must shape a new mentality in America. Man's desires must overshadow his needs.

It wasn't until after a Great Depression and World War II that Mazur's words would prove prophetic – but there's no denying that they form an accurate description of the way we buy and consume things in large parts of the world today. In other words: we no longer just buy products because of their practical, primary value (because we *need* them) but because of their semantic, secondary value: their ability to shape our identities and the way they make us feel. As ironic as it might sound, we distinguish ourselves from the masses by buying mass-produced goods. Consider this famous former Apple slogan: "Think Different." The message here verges on the absurd: "Want to be different? Join the ever-growing group of customers of one of the biggest multinationals in the world!"

This model has proven to be an effective way to get people to consume an endless procession of stuff throughout their lives, leaving tons and tons of waste behind. The enormous influence of fashion and trends on our desires is exerted mainly through a sheer-omnipresent media culture, which can hardly be escaped. The meaning of the symbols we use to construct our identities change all the time, and we are painfully aware of those changes. So-called "fast fashion," a trend which developed in the recent years, makes the pace in which this happens even worse. Every second the equivalent of one truckload of clothes is landfilled or burned, representing a $500 billion value, which is lost annually due to clothing that is barely worn and rarely recycled. Fashion trends often also go along with social pressure, notably for children. Our son's football shoes represented something he would happily be associated with one year; a year later, however, they mean something altogether different: they're totally *uncool*. Within a single year, the same pair of shoes translates into the opposite identity. *They were designed to become uncool.*

The motor behind this business model is the high speed that characterizes fashion cycles, which rigorously shuffle the links between products and symbols. That means that if consumers wish to maintain the same symbolic value, they are forced to buy new products continuously. Manufacturers consequently focus more on these symbolic aspects than on the intrinsic quality of products. The most obvious example for this kind of planned obsolescence is, of course, the world of fashion, which has built an entire industry around this form of psychological manipulation, and whose influence – helped by the rise of extremely cheap budget-manufacturers such as Primark – continues to shrink the life span of items of clothing. Fast-fashion brands like Zara and H&M now offer around 20 different collections per year, instead of

one each season.[26] The number of times a garment is worn decreased
by at least 36% over the past few decades at the global level, but for
affluent countries, the numbers are even more striking: in the US,
clothes are only worn for around a quarter of the global average, and
in China, clothing utilization decreased by 70%. At the same time,
global clothing production has doubled. Large amounts of energy, water
and other resources are needed to make all those clothes: the fashion
industry contributes to 10% of global greenhouse gas emissions and the
production of one single kilogram of garment uses 20.000 liters of water.
Meanwhile 73% of the total annual feed-stock is landfilled and only 1% of
the material is recycled into new clothing.[27] "Clothing production is the
third biggest manufacturing industry after the automotive and technology
industries," reads a 2019 House of Commons Environmental Audit
Committee report on the topic and goes on to say: "Textile production
contributes more to climate change than international aviation and
shipping combined."[28]

A NATURAL CARTEL

Planned obsolescence, whether realized through technical, functional
or psychological manipulation, is a successful business model that
encourages and speeds up the sale of products; but it is not without cost
for consumers and the environment. The amount of products for sale
is continuously on the rise, while the life span of the average product
has been decreasing steadily. Researchers at the Rochester Institute of
Technology found that the life span of an average computer has decreased
by almost two-thirds in the past few decades.[29] In 1985, a PC computer
would last an average of 10.7 years, by 2000, this number had halved;
according to *The Guardian*, the average life span today is between 3
and 5 years.[30] The share of large household appliances that had to be
replaced within the first five years of use has more than doubled between
2004 and 2013.[31] According to 2019 data from tens of thousands of
consumer reports collected by the website consumerreports.org, 40% of

all refrigerators today develop problems within the first five years of their life span.[32]

Agreements between companies hardly surprise us, these days. The rules of the planned obsolescence business models have become normal, we take them for granted; they have simply become an integral part of the accepted corporate and consumer culture. And while this situation sounds significantly less mysterious than a secret conspiracy story, it's a lot more effective. A controversial, enigmatic cartel is quite a primitive form of behavior control, after all. Secret rules and deals have to be made, not to mention all the people needed to enforce these rules. Most importantly, the necessity of these agreements (secret rules, secret deals) means that the people involved can still imagine a different situation.

Behavior regulation is most efficient when people have internalized certain principles so thoroughly that they cannot even conceive of a situation different from the one they find themselves in. What makes psychological power (the power of those ideas that have become standard parts of a culture) so forceful is exactly that inconspicuousness. As the Korean-German philosopher Byung-Chul Han states in his book *Psychopolitics:*

> Considerably more efficient [than external power] is the kind of power that causes people to make themselves inferior to their context *voluntarily*. Its special efficiency originates in the fact that it does not make use of prohibition and denial, but of gratification and fulfillment. In an environment in which power is not considered a special theme, it is undeniably present.[33]

This also brings us to the oft-heard remark that consumer demand is the driving force behind the throwaway society, an argument which certainly cannot be fully dismissed. Yet the fundamental question remains: who educated whom? Going back to the cigarette example: obviously every individual has the free choice of deciding to smoke a cigarette, but only a great cynic would be able to argue that the fact he or she does has nothing to do with the heavy marketing investments of the tobacco industry: $1 million per hour in the US alone!

Even if consumers are conscious, it remains difficult to make the right choices. The lack of transparency created by the industry concerning technical life span or reparability makes it impossible for consumers to make an informed choice. Saturated markets especially are characterized by a high number of product types, constant changes in design and functional specifications, and a flood of information and marketing. It does not come as a surprise that a new research area has emerged over the last decades, referred to as 'consumer confusion.'

By making planned obsolescence a standard part of the world of production and consumption, the manufacturer's problem has been successfully shifted: in the short term, toward the individual consumer, in the long term, to the entire society, in the form of a throwaway culture that destroys the only inhabitable physical environment we have. As much as we have finally become aware of the problems that threaten our living conditions, we remain largely blind to the role played by planned obsolescence.

All three of the business models mentioned above enlarge the gap between the performance cycle (how long we want to use a product) and the life cycle (how long it takes for the product to break down). In our current system, that gap results in an astonishing amount of *waste*, either caused by continuous 'improvement' or a well-planned lack thereof. The consumer, society and the planet suffer the consequences of engineering decisions solely motivated by the goal of maximizing the manufacturer's profits. Of course: manufacturers need to make profit. The question that

THE WAY WE CONSUME

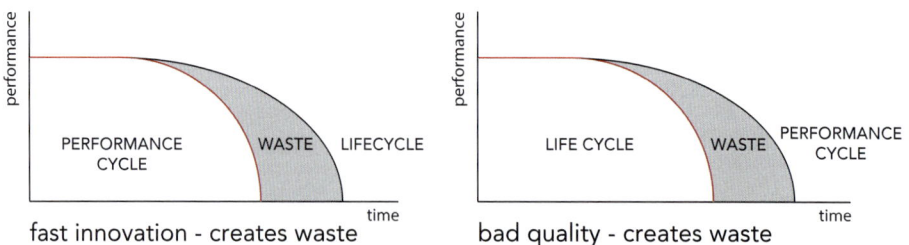

fast innovation - creates waste

bad quality - creates waste

CHAPTER ONE: THE PRODUCT-AS-PROBLEM

should be asked, however, is the following: is it really only possible to make profit *at the expense* of someone or something else?

MURKS? NEIN DANKE

In our shed are still tools we have inherited from our grandparents. Even after decades and decades of use, they still function perfectly. There's a chain of stores in Germany that sells tools of comparable quality: at Manufactum (Es gibt sie noch, die guten Dinge), you can still find products that outlive fashion and trends, products built to last for generations. Their tools are made from sustainable materials, always designed with care. Of course, the price is a bit higher than usual, but take into consideration that you will have to buy these products just once in your lifetime and you'll find that they're actually quite cheap. The chain's tagline therefore is "Billig is uns zu teuer" ("cheap is too expensive for us").

That also happens to be the motto of German business economist Stefan Schridde, who has been trying to spur up debate about planned obsolescence in Germany for years. Schridde is the founder of a citizens' movement called *Murks? Nein Danke* (Short-cut-goods? No Thanks), an organization that encourages consumers to report unsound equipment, and which tries to use claims and court cases to force manufacturers to produce responsibly and sustainably. According to the organization's calculations, roughly a €50 billion would be saved every year by German consumers alone, if planned obsolescence would be halved.

The organization also points out that an average European consumes about 43 kilo of natural resources a day, contrasted by a mere 10 kilo per person in Africa. The average American citizen, meanwhile, consumes no less than 90 kilo a day. In the meantime worldwide resource extraction has more than tripled over the past 50 years while population only doubled in the same period: about 92 billion tons of raw materials are extracted per year. Given current trends of growth, our extraction of natural resources would increase to 190 billion tons by 2060.[34]

29

There are, of course, more initiatives and also some manufacturers that are trying to turn the tide. Consider *Phoneblocks*, for instance: an organization that advocates the development of devices made up of easily separable components, allowing consumers to simply purchase the component that needs replacement rather than a whole new device.[35]

In addition, the web is full of online marketplace sites, which invite people to put their used products up for sale. And even when it comes to the psychological manipulation of the advertising business, there is no lack of counter-movements, such as the UK-based anti-advertising movement *Brandalism*: an international street art collective that mobilizes artists around the world to take 'creative action' against the abundance of ads in public space.[36]

The initiative of *Repair Cafés*, which started in the Netherlands in 2009, is currently present in 35 countries.[37] The initiative organizes regular meetings in which volunteers repair a great variety of products from household appliances, to computers and clothes. There is even a Silicon Valley version of this initiative called *I-Fixit*, which provides online repair manuals and sells tools, encouraging consumers to repair their own devices. However, a fierce fight is being fought in the US for this very right. With the argument that repair information is proprietary, manufacturers try to prevent consumers from taking care for their own goods. In 2019, 20 US states have introduced the Right to Repair laws, but the legislation has not been implemented yet in any of them.[38]

But governments are also acting: in Sweden, repairs are being exempted from VAT and the labor costs involved can be deducted from the tax bill. Italy and France have passed legislation against planned obsolescence. As a matter of fact, Italy's competition authority has issued fines of €10m and €5m, respectively, to phone manufacturers Apple and Samsung for cutting down the performance of specific models following a software update.[39]

As heartening as these initiatives, battles and policies are, however, none of them alone qualifies as a long-term solution. Why not? Because they still operate within a linear economic system, in which products ultimately end up as waste and power and responsibility reside in very different places: on opposite sides of the system. The consequences of decisions taken by *manufacturers*, in all these cases, are still passed on to *consumers*; and in the long term to the only planet we have.

NOTES

1 Kettering, C. (1929). "The key to economic prosperity…" quoted from The End of Work (1995) by Jeremy Rifkin, p. 19.
2 Livermore's Centennial Light Bulb. (2021). https://www.centennialbulb.org
3 Marcuse, H. (1991). *One-dimensional man: Studies in the ideology of advanced industrial society.* Boston, MA: Beacon Press.
4 Krajewski, M. (2014). *The great lightbulb conspiracy.* IEEE Spectrum. https://spectrum.ieee.org/tech-history/dawn-of-electronics/the-great-lightbulb-conspiracy
5 Dannoritzer, C. (2010). *The light bulb conspiracy.* https://topdocumentaryfilms.com/light-bulb-conspiracy/
6 Kreiß, C. (2001). *Geplanter Verschleiß: Wie die Industrie uns zu immer mehr und immer schnellerem Konsum antreibt – und wie wir uns dagegen wehren können.* Berlin: Europaverlag.
7 Pynchon, T. (1973). *Gravity's rainbow.* New York: Viking Press.
8 London, B. (1932). *Ending the depression through planned obsolescence.* https://www.semanticscholar.org/paper/Ending-the-Depression-through-Planned-Obsolescence-London/622892147cfe3c4567d0d92d528394423d93e5a4
9 Glenn A. (2003). *Industrial strength design: How Brooks Stevens shaped your world.* Cambridge, Mass.: MIT Press.
10 Appliance Spare Parts Availability and the Law. (2012, updated 2016). https://www.ukwhitegoods.co.uk/help/spare-parts/general-spare-part-help/3473-appliance-spare-parts-and-the-law
11 Brönneke, T., & Wechsler, A. (2015). *Obsoleszenz interdisziplinär,* Schriftenreihe des Instituts für Europäisches Wirtschafts-und Verbraucheerrecht e.V. Band 37, Baden-Baden.
12 Connexion (2018). 'Built-in obsolescence' study targets women's tights. Retrieved from https://www.connexionfrance.com/French-news/Built-in-obsolescence-study-targets-women-s-tights

13 They Time Those Things, designforlongevity.com. https://designforlongevity.com/videos/they-time-those-things

14 Eco@Work (2016). *Obsolescence, causes, effects, strategies.* Oeko Institut Germany. https://www.oeko.de/fileadmin/magazin/2016/02/ecoatwork_02_2016_en.pdf

15 European Environment Agency (2020). *Europe's consumption in a circular economy: The benefits of longer-lasting electronics.* https://www.eea.europa.eu/publications/europe2019s-consumption-in-a-circular/benefits-of-longer-lasting-electronics

16 Roser, M. (2019). *Working hours.* OurWorldInData.org. https://ourworldindata.org/working-hours

17 Ip, G. (2016). *The economy's hidden problem: We're out of big ideas.* https://www.wsj.com/articles/the-economys-hidden-problem-were-out-of-big-ideas-1481042066

18 Sloan, A. P. (1972). *My years with general motors*/Garden City, NY: Doubleday.

19 Prakash, S., Schleicher, T., Dehoust, G., Gsell, M., & Stamminger, R. (2016): *Einfluss der Nutzungsdauer von Produkten auf ihre Umweltwirkung: Schaffung einer Informationsgrundlage und Entwicklung von Strategien gegen "Obsoleszenz".* Study by Ökoinstitut commission by the German Umweltbundesamt, Retrieved from: https://www.umweltbundesamt.de/sites/default/files/medien/378/publikation/texte_11_2016_einfluss_der_nutzungsdauer_von_produkten_obsoleszenz.pdf

20 Simon Kucher & Partners (2019). *Relevance and future users of Apple TV+.* https://www.simon-kucher.com/nl/about/media-center/new-study-streaming-services-rapidly-replacing-traditional-tv

21 Gartner (2017). Market Share: PCs, Ultramobiles and Mobile Phones, All Countries, 4Q17.

22 Gartner Press Release (2021). 'Gartner Says Worldwide Smartphone Sales to Grow 11% by 2021. https://www.gartner.com/en/newsroom/press-releases/2021-02-03-gartner-says-worldwide-smartphone-sales-to-grow-11-percent-in-2021

23 U.S. Geological Survey (2006). *Recycled cell phones – A treasure trove of valuable metals.* Fact Sheet 2006-3097, Department of Interior, July. https://pubs.usgs.gov/fs/2006/3097/fs2006-3097.pdf

24 Electronics Take Back Coalition (2014). *Facts and figures on e-waste and recycling,* http://www.electronicstakeback.com/wp-content/uploads/Facts_and_Figures_on_EWaste_and_Recycling.pdf

25 Curtis, A. (2002). *The century of the self.* BBC documentary series.

26 Remy, N., Speelman, E., & Swartz, S. (2016). *Style that's sustainable: A new fast-fashion formula.* McKinsey. https://www.mckinsey.com/business-functions/sustainability/our-insights/style-thats-sustainable-a-new-fast-fashion-formula

27 EllenMacArthurFoundation (2017). *A new textiles economy.* https://www.ellenmacarthurfoundation.org/assets/downloads/A-New-Textiles-Economy_Full-Report_Updated_1-12-17.pdf

28 House of Commons Environmental Audit Committee (2019). *Fixing fashion: Clothing consumption and sustainability.* https://publications.parliament.uk/pa/cm201719/cmselect/cmenvaud/1952/1952.pdf

29 Babbitt, C. W., Kahhat, R., Williams, E., & Babbitt, G. A. (2009). "Evolution of product lifespan and implications for environmental assessment and management: A case study of personal computers in higher education." *Environmental Science & Technology*, Vol. 43, No. 13, pp. 5106–5112.

30 Siegle, L. (2013). *What is the lifespan of a laptop?* The Guardian environment https://www.theguardian.com/environment/2013/jan/13/lifespan-laptop-pc-planned-obsolescence

31 Geere, D. (2016). Electronic product lifespans are getting shorter. https://www.wired.co.uk/article/product-lifespans

32 Consumer Reports (2019). *How long will your appliance last?* https://www.consumerreports.org/appliances/how-long-will-your-appliances-last/

33 Han, B.-C. (2017). *Psychopolitics: Neoliberalism and new technologies of power.* London: Verso Books.

34 IRP (2019). *Global resources outlook 2019: Natural resources for the future we want.* Oberle, B., Bringezu, S., Hatfeld-Dodds, S., Hellweg, S., Schandl, H., Clement, J., Cabernard, L., Che, N., Chen, D., Droz-Georget, H., Ekins, P., FischerKowalski, M., Flörke, M., Frank, S., Froemelt, A., Geschke, A., Haupt, M., Havlik, P., Hüfner, R., Lenzen, M., Lieber, M., Liu, B., Lu, Y., Lutter, S., Mehr, J., Miatto, A., Newth, D., Oberschelp, C., Obersteiner, M., Pfster, S., Piccoli, E., Schaldach, R., Schüngel, J., Sonдеregger, T., Sudheshwar, A., Tanikawa, H., van der Voet, E., Walker, C., West, J., Wang, Z., Zhu, B. *A report of the international resource panel.* Nairobi, Kenya: United Nations Environment Programme.

35 Phonebloks: https://phonebloks.com

36 Brandalism: http://brandalism.ch

37 Repaircafé: https://repaircafe.org/en/visit/

38 We Have the Right to Repair Everything We Own, Ifixit: https://www.ifixit.com/Right-to-Repair/Intro

39 *BBC News* (2018). *Apple and Samsung fined by Italian authorities over slow phones.* BBC News, https://www.bbc.com/news/technology-45963943

You cannot escape the responsibility of tomorrow by evading it today.

(ABRAHAM LINCOLN)

CHAPTER TWO

The linear economy or *the end of the line*

The linear economy turns raw materials into waste at an ever-increasing pace. Reports about future resource scarcity are piling up, but change is only coming slow if it comes at all. Why are we not acting faster, and what can be done to turn the tide?

DOI: 10.4324/9781003258674-3

On March 13, 1964, a young woman named Catherine 'Kitty' Genovese departed her car near Queens, New York City, in a parking lot surrounded by flats. It was late; a quarter past three in the morning. She was returning from her job as a waitress. A few minutes earlier, however, she had been spotted by Winston Moseley: a 29-year-old machinist who followed her home. As soon as she got out of her car in the parking lot, Moseley ran toward her and stabbed her twice in the back with a knife. She screamed for help.

Kitty was heard by a handful of people. One man yelled something from his window, upon which the machinist quickly ran back to his car. When no one came down to help her, however, Moseley went after her again. Once more Moseley was interrupted by some yelling residents. But as soon as their voices died away again, he continued his pursuit. He caught up with Kitty in the flat's entrance hall and resumed his attack. She died on the spot. Not until ten minutes to four did one of the flat residents call the police. Moseley had had 35 minutes to kill his victim.

A newspaper article describing this incident reported that a total of 38 flat residents had seen or at least heard the attack on Kitty Genovese. Not one of them, however, had made any effort to help her. Nobody had even called the police until it was too late. The article resulted in public outrage, and ultimately in an extensive study looking at possible psychological explanations for what had happened – or failed to happen.[1]

THE DIFFUSION OF RESPONSIBILITY

Kitty's story later became a famous example of what social psychologists have named the *bystander effect*: a phenomenon that occurs when a group of individuals share responsibility for the solution to a problem. The bystander effect, in turn, is caused by a phenomenon called 'the diffusion of responsibility.' When this phenomenon occurs, the experienced responsibility for whatever is happening is spread out over all the people in the group. Each individual member of the group therefore experiences only a highly diluted sense of responsibility. Often, the result is that not a single member of the group interferes with the situation.[2]

What this phenomenon emphasizes is the importance of the relation between action and experienced responsibility; the first presupposes the second. If we don't feel responsible for a situation, we're not inclined to try and change it. Experiencing responsibility, in turn, presupposes that one feels some degree of power over the events unfolding. If someone feels that their influence on a given situation is negligible, they will experience little incentive to take action. Yet, this feeling of power is highly individual and is referred to by psychologists with the term self-efficacy. Self-efficacy is an individual's belief in his or her innate ability to achieve goals. Stanford psychologist Albert Bandura defines it as a personal judgment of "how well one can execute courses of action required to deal with prospective situations."

With this in mind, try to answer the following question. What happens when the ability to act and the formal responsibility for a situation have been separated entirely? Person A acts, but formally passes on the responsibility for the situation to person B, in effect 'making' person B responsible. Person B, however, does not really have any power over the situation, so he or she doesn't experience that responsibility.

It's simple enough to see that the problem would probably persist eternally, or perhaps until it transforms from being a problem into an irreversible catastrophe. Still, this is exactly how we deal with power and responsibility in our current economic model, allowing the consequences of our linear production chain to rapidly turn into planet-wide catastrophes.

THE END-OF-THE-LINE

Imagine a manufacturer who is allowed to sell responsibility (along with television sets, blenders, cross trainers and diapers), a linear production chain and, near the end of the line, a consumer who hardly has any knowledge of the production process; let alone power to influence it. The result? Staggering amounts of waste.

Our current production chain is organized so that nobody ever really needs to take responsibility for the consequences of their actions. Responsibility is passed on throughout the chain and sold as easily as though it was just a minor detail in the transaction. This goes on until the product ends up in anonymity, in a giant heap of waste: the end of the line. The consequences are being born by Nature or people far away from the place where the products were consumed.

As soon as a product arrives at this terminal station, its particular features and characteristics dissolve to make way for a new, rather undistinguished identity: that of *waste*, an identity that renders all products equal – that is to say: equally worthless. Because as soon as a product loses its identity, all knowledge of the materials it consists of, as well as its individual potential for re-use, have been lost.

The last link before this irreversible step is the consumer: the gatekeeper who decides whether a product or material is doomed or given another chance to live, so to speak. Consumers are hopelessly unequipped for that role, however. They have little or no knowledge about the materials used in production, the technical decisions that were made, or possible forms of re-use and above all – no single means to influence any of it. When consumers buy a light bulb, they're unaware that it was designed to break down after a 1,000 hours. They have limited knowledge about the natural resources that have been used for its production, or whether the production process has been sustainable and/or socially responsible. As to the materials left in the bulb when they are about to toss it into the bin: 99% of consumers have no idea of what they are.

To make consumers the people in charge of a product's fate is thus irresponsible; in the entire production chain, they are by far least likely to make the right decision.

The result of this model is that most products end up as waste. The manufacturer's problem, as described in the previous chapter, is thus transformed from a threat to business revenues into a threat to living conditions. The power to influence the production process and the responsibility for its consequences are separated from each other by the distance of an entire 'production chain'; meet *the linear economy*.

THE LAUNDERING MACHINE

Of course, consumers are not entirely unaware of the fact that the products they buy (may) have been manufactured in socially irresponsible circumstances or by means of production processes that form a serious threat to the environment. On the contrary, consumers are more conscious than ever of the fact that their behavior as consumers affects people, animals and natural environments all over the world. But this development hasn't resulted in any big changes in consumer behavior or in significant outbreaks of public revolt. No demonstrations against dire working conditions in Bangladeshi sweatshops, no masses of people taking their money out of the custody of banks that indirectly use their savings to finance bloody conflicts, no large-scale consumer boycotts. Why not?

The answer is that even though modern consumers have access to more and more information about the interdependence that characterizes today's global economy (and thus their own direct contribution to the problems they read about), their daily lives take place in a world that displays no traces of injustice; no sign of environmental destruction, underpaid workers, child soldiers or animal maltreatment. We have been separated from these things entirely, by the complete linear production chain as well as clever marketing and the ever-growing complexity of the networks of global trade. We do not associate our supermarket-bought steak, convenient internet banking system, our smartphone or new dress with any of the issues described above.

That is one of the most impressive feats of the combined forces of the linear economy, modern-day marketing and globalization. Together they function as a sort of laundering-machine: no matter how destructive, shocking or cruel the first few links of the production chain may have been, further on in the chain, the same shiny, innocent-looking products will come rolling off the conveyor belt. Products that bear no trace whatsoever of illegal logging, destructive pollution or child labor.

This undermines feelings of responsibility consumers might otherwise experience. The actions and the responsibility for those actions have thus been so utterly separated that in the end nobody feels prompted to try to change something. And the global scale of this issue makes matters worse, in the form of a worldwide bystander effect.

FREE-ROAMING OR FREE-FARMED?

Even when consumers do feel responsible, the complex interconnected web of global supply chains has made it almost impossible for consumers to know what the 'right' thing to do is. For example: consumers who follow a vegan diet, out of a sense of responsibility for the environment and the welfare of their fellow beings on Earth, often consume milk made of almonds instead of milk extracted from cows. In recent years, it has become known, however, that 90% of almond-growing companies in California (where 80% of the world's almonds are grown) have to physically import bee colonies to pollinate the almond trees. According to the Pollinator Stewardship Council, "somewhere between 15 and 25 percent of the beehives in almond groves suffered severe damage during the bloom, ranging from complete hive collapse to dead and deformed brood." This is caused by the pesticides and fungicides utilized in the almond groves, plus the week-long transport on trucks.[3] A well-intentioned consumer decision informed by a sense of responsibility for the environment and animals, in today's complicated world, can result in the deaths of large numbers of the animals that play a more vital role in sustaining our lives on Earth than any other animal on the planet.

Meanwhile, the jungle of well-intended labels we come across in the supermarket does more to confuse us than to help us navigate: according to the Ecolabel Index, the largest global directory of eco-labels, there currently exist 455 different eco-labels in 199 countries and 25 industry sectors.[4] How are we to know which ones to trust? Should we buy free-roaming or free-farmed eggs? Grass-fed, antibiotic-free or biodynamic? Even the most devoted environmentalist might be forgiven for making the wrong choice here. "It's like the wild west," said Gay Browne, founder and chief executive officer (CEO) of an online database and independent rating system of green businesses to *The Guardian*. "Too many labels offer weak or unsubstantiated claims and many amount to little more than self-declarations made by individual companies."[5]

On the one hand, we can thus distinguish groups of consumers whose sense of responsibility is significantly weakened by the complexity of the global supply chain network and the powers of advertising, while on the other hand, we can distinguish groups of consumers who do feel responsible, but for whom, it appears to be sheerly impossible to know which decision will lead to the desired results – and not to a whole range of unforeseen effects that amount to more destruction than their well-intentioned decision was supposed to prevent in the first place.

It should therefore be clear that consumers, lacking crucial information and power over the production process and the long chain of supply behind it, are not equipped to handle the responsibilities loaded onto them by today's linear economy. It's a fundamental rule: power and responsibility need to stay together. Separate the two and things will inevitably go amiss. Just think about the escalated financial gambling practices that led to the worldwide financial crisis of 2008: the people involved were able to take gigantic risks, since the accountability for what would happen next was rendered so diffuse (by intricate financial products) that it was pretty much negligible. That did not, however, make the resulting events any less damaging to the global economy, and individual lives all over the world.

TAKE, MAKE, WASTE

In the 1920s, when the Phoebus cartel was founded, planned obsolescence may have seemed like a sensible solution to the manufacturer's problem. Even though people by then rationally knew that the Earth and her resources were exhaustible, the limits of this closed system were still so far away that this fact did not seem to pose an urgent problem; there was little awareness about the finite nature of

the conditions that make our lives possible, and the attitude connected to imperialism and colonialism were still in bloom; when one place was drained of its fruits, people just moved on to the next. The limits of our planet's ecosystem were still invisible, which created an illusion of infinity.

The publication of the report 'The Limits to Growth' by the Club of Rome in 1972 gave rise to the first moment in history during which we seemed to fully realize that there are borders, that our environment is fragile and that our raw material deposits are exhaustible.[6] In addition, it taught us that our actions affect the environment much more than we could ever imagine. Yet today, nearly half a century later, we still live as though the sky is our only limit (if that).

We are stuck with a one-dimensional economic model: the linear economy. We mine raw materials, turn them into goods, use those goods for a while and throw them out. End of story. The consequence of consumption in this model is always the same: waste. The linear economy is, therefore, frequently referred to as the take, make and waste economy. This would have been bad enough if it had not been sped up by planned obsolescence from the first half of the twentieth century, but the fact is that it has. The incredible speed with which we turn the world's resources into trash is a direct consequence of the planned obsolescence business models – not a coincidental correlation. The Global E-waste Monitor 2020, a report produced in collaboration with the UN Environmental Program (UNEP), found that a record 53.6 million metric tons of electronic waste was generated in 2019. That is the weight of more than a million 50-ton transportation trucks; more than enough to fill three times a line of trucks the distance between Frankfurt to Tokyo. Representing a value of approximately ¢57 billion US dollar![7]

QUANTIFYING NATURE?

There is only one dimension in which the logic underpinning planned obsolescence makes sense, and that is in the short-term financial dimension. The objective of this business model, after all, is to generate financial profit for the manufacturer of a product: nothing else is taken into account. The costs are outsourced and not easy to capture in monetary terms, so they never show up on the manufacturer's balance. Indeed, they do not enter the financial dimension at all, until they have become irreversible. They are paid for by individual consumers, society and the natural world, in the form of destructive pollution, the exhaustion of natural resource supplies and the effects of climate change. In short: profits are privatized, costs are socialized.

Some undoubtedly well-intentioned initiatives try to pull these so-called external costs into the financial dimension. In 2007, for example, research initiative The Economics of Ecosystems and Biodiversity (TEEB) was created upon the request of the environment ministers from the G8+5 meeting in Potsdam, Germany. This initiative aims to make the services provided by ecosystems and biodiversity – such as clean air – financially measurable, so that it is possible to weigh them against financial profits. In addition, TEEB aims to quantify the costs of the loss of biodiversity and the failure to take protective measures versus the costs of effective conservation.[8]

A similar approach is pursued by Full Cost or True Cost accounting, which seeks to consider not only the usual financial values of goods and services, but also their impact on natural and social capital. These effects too are communicated in monetary terms and printed in euros, so that the amounts can be included in the financial reporting. The hidden costs of entrepreneurial activities, which are usually externalized, are thus made visible and included in the balance sheets.

However well-intentioned these initiatives might be, they are also somewhat absurd: Nature has no price tag. The costs they attempt to quantify touch the most fundamental conditions for our lives on this planet, which need to be secured before we can think of purchasing anything money can buy us. Pulling them into the financial dimension can be practical in the sense that it makes them more tangible and easier to weigh against financial profits. For instance, the Food and Agriculture Organization of the United Nations found that the external costs of global production of maize, rice, soybean and wheat are 1.7 times higher than their product value.[9]

Assessing these external costs in monetary terms, however, also creates the false impression that they can be contained by this narrow dimension of balances and currencies. In reality, the most valuable of ecosystem services have unlimited value, and no known alternatives. They both transcend and form the most existential condition for our world of finances and economics.

In addition, all valuation of Nature is subjective: whose priorities will determine the value of our environment? Our societies and economies seem confused enough about the distinction between 'value' and 'financial value' – and initiatives like TEEB and True Cost accounting only seem to add to this confusion. Financially quantifying external costs might pave the way for the marketization and privatization of Nature.

A TICKING TIME BOMB

Consumers have very little choice: when they buy a product, they immediately become the owners of that product and thus responsible for what will happen to it and how this will affect our planet. Ownership could thus be characterized as a form of risk-taking. While we can avoid certain personal risks, however (by abstaining from alcohol and cigarettes, or keeping our savings in our bank account rather than making risky investments), it is very difficult to avoid ownership in today's world. The average person nowadays owns several million products throughout their lifetime, from private jets and houses to toothpicks and bus tickets.

The supply of raw materials needed for the production of all those products is finite. A linear economy will thus inevitably lead to its exhaustion – in theory, at least. In practice, materials will never truly 'run out.' As soon as a material becomes so scarce that exhaustion can be considered an imminent threat, its price will increase so much that manufacturers will simply be forced to stop using the material in question for the production of their goods, because it will not be economically viable to do so.

Already in 2011, PricewaterhouseCoopers published a report in which it called the impending worldwide resource shortage a 'ticking time bomb' for the world's biggest manufacturing industries. 'Put simply,' its sustainability leader Malcolm Preston said, "many businesses now recognise that we are living beyond the planet's means. New business models will be fundamental to the ability to respond appropriately to the risks and opportunities posed by the scarcity of minerals and metals." From this point of view alone, the fact that we are turning valuable scarce material into non-recyclable waste is utterly incomprehensible.[10]

The gigantic economic growth that has characterized our societies ever since the industrial revolution has accelerated this process to a mind-blowing extent, and its speed is still increasing. We believe, therefore, that the image of a ticking time bomb is an accurate one, although this bomb is more likely to implode than explode. The construction industry, which as a sector consumes around 40% of global resources, provides a staggering example: in just the three years 2011–2013, the amount of cement used in China was equaled to the amount used in the United States in the entire twentieth century.[11] The amount of available raw materials is decreasing in proportion to the exponential growth of fast-growing economies like China.

The specter of Peak Mineral looms over our industries: the moment in time from which supply of 'terrestrial ores' can no longer rise to meet demand – a moment that has passed already for some minerals.[12] According to several studies, the deposits of many metals and metal ores will be consumed within the current century. This is especially true for many rare minerals that are indispensable for, among other things, the production of smartphones, wind turbines, computers and batteries. Cobalt and lithium shortages are already a fact manufacturers have to deal with. But even the proverbial sand in our oceans is becoming scarce. The global urbanization boom devours enormous amounts of sand, which is the key ingredient of concrete and asphalt. "Just about every apartment block, skyscraper, office tower and shopping mall that gets built anywhere from Beijing to Lagos is made with concrete, which is essentially just sand and gravel glued together with cement," journalist Vince Beiser wrote in *The Guardian* in 2017.[13] "Every yard of asphalt road that connects those buildings is also made of sand. So is every window in every one of those buildings." Because desert sand is not suitable for building, however, coasts and river mouths worldwide are threatened by so-called sand mining, which causes severe environmental damage. In Indonesia, the practice of sand mining has already caused entire islands to disappear from the map.

Even from the one-dimensional, financial perspective, the logic underpinning planned obsolescence will thus soon start to waver, when manufacturers will be bereft of the continuous supply of materials that are vital to their production processes. When, eventually, the price of these materials will have increased so much that manufacturers can no longer use them to make a profit, products get replaced by newer versions that can be made with different raw materials – which, of course, can keep the wasteful economic model going for a while longer, while also exhausting some other precious resource. But if nothing has been done to secure the accessibility of previously extracted materials the linear production chain will collapse – taking its exploitative business models down with it.

LOCKED UP?

The irreversible exhaustion of our planet's materials is not a *potential* outcome of the linear production chain; as long as we're confined to an environment characterized by finitude, it is logically inherent to it. In spite of this, efforts to change the system are either half-hearted or downright opposed by industry. We might obediently sort our waste and try to recycle certain things, but these are at best half-measures, and very far from enough. For example: of the 53.6 million metric tons of e-waste generated worldwide in 2019, only 17.4% was officially documented as properly collected and recycled.[14] Even when products are in fact recycled, only a fraction of the value of the original material remains intact, a process referred to as 'downcycling.' Our products and processes are not designed to facilitate the process of material recovery.

Recycling in its current form is thus not a solution to the problems described above: at most, it can put them off just a little longer. The same applies to other methods for the recovery of raw materials: at best, they slow down the process of decline. They are, however, incapable of turning the tide, because the actual problem goes much deeper. And as with any other problem or disease, just fighting symptoms will do nothing to solve it. Indeed, in most cases, (as in this case) symptom fighting even *adds* to the problem; it withdraws attention from underlying causes, which is potentially riskier than doing nothing at all.

If our GP would react to our medical complaints by just giving us some painkillers, without having displayed the slightest curiosity regarding the potential cause of our pain, we would feel understandably indignant. In fact, we would probably switch to a different practitioner, rather than swallow some aspirin and hope for the best. Still, we don't seem to mind this approach when it's applied to the health of our environment which is, after all, a fundamental condition for the existence of everything else: business models, products and GPs alike.

The question is: how do we leave our current path, which we know will lead only to destruction and decline? How do we rid ourselves of these limited business models, excessive overconsumption and mountains of waste?

THE NEED FOR DECOUPLING

Once upon a time, there was a law against planned obsolescence; GDR law stated that products had to last for *at least 25 years*. This measure was motivated by neither idealism nor environmental concern. East Germany was simply cut off from the West and therefore unable to enjoy the free traffic of goods and capital that characterizes a capitalist system; the assortment of products in most shops was as limited as the financial resources of the average citizen. The East German government therefore decided to make sure that the products that were produced were of outstanding quality. Naturally, manufacturers were held responsible for this – not consumers. Of course, we are far from advocating a return to those times! The only lesson we can draw from this anecdote is that it is possible to make long-lasting products, some of the old GDR household appliances still work, decades after the state ceased to exist.[15]

Of course, nothing lasts forever. No matter how fantastic, every product is finite. We are, however, perfectly capable of doubling the lifetime of our products, *many times over*. Either by making them more sustainable or by designing them in such a way that they can be repaired or that the components they consist of can be easily replaced or retrieved and processed into other products. How do we get there? We need to stop facilitating our current, destructive business models and decouple economic growth from the exploitation of raw materials.

Changing fiscal incentives, for instance, could be a first important step. For a number of years now, experts have been advocating a tax reform: shifting from taxing labor to taxing final resources in the form of energy and material. This would lower the costs of repairs and material recovery and incentivize businesses to focus on resource efficiency rather than searching labor-related efficiency gains. Sweden's decision to lower VAT for repairs is a very important step in this direction.

Most importantly, however, we need to reunite the *possibility to act* with the *responsibility for the consequences of those actions*. Those who decide about production-processes have also the duty to manage their long-term consequences, and must be prevented from selling and reselling their responsibility throughout the linear production chain – all the way to the end of the line. In order for this to happen, we need to change the rules of the game and introduce business models with a future. One of these rules could be that producers should hold on to their products and sell them as a service instead.

NOTES

1 Cook, K. (2014). *Kitty Genovese: The murder, the bystanders, the crime that changed America.* New York: W. W. Norton & Company.

2 *Diffusion of Responsibility. Encyclopædia Britannica*, Encyclopædia Britannica, Inc. https://www.britannica.com/topic/bystander-effect/Diffusion-of-responsibility

3 Philpott, T (2014). *Are your delicious, healthy almonds killing bees?* Mother Jones. https://www.motherjones.com/food/2014/04/california-almond-farms-blamed-honeybee-die/

4 Ecolabel Index. http://www.ecolabelindex.com/

5 Atkinson, L. (2014). *Wild west' of eco-labels: Sustainability claims are confusing consumers.* The Guardian, Guardian News and Media. https://www.theguardian.com/sustainable-business/eco-labels-sustainability-trust-corporate-government

6 Meadows, D. H. [and others]. (1972). *The limits to growth; a report for the Club of Rome's project on the predicament of mankind.* New York: Universe Books.

7 Forti, V., Baldé, C. P., Kuehr, R., & Bel, G. (2020) The Global E-waste Monitor 2020. http://ewastemonitor.info/

8 The Economics of Ecosystems and Biodiversity (TEEB) is a global initiative focused on "making nature's values visible". Its principal objective is to mainstream the values of biodiversity and ecosystem services into decision-making at all levels. https://www.teebweb.org

9 FAO (2017). *The future of food and agriculture – Trends and challenges.* Rome. http://www.fao.org/3/a-i6583e.pdf

10 PriceWaterhouseCooper (2011). *Minerals and metals scarcity in manufacturing: The ticking time bomb.* https://www.pwc.com/ua/en/industry/metal_mining/assets/impact_of_minerals_metals_scarcity_on_business.pdf

11 McCarthy, N. (2014). China Used More Concrete in 3 Years than the U.S. Used in the Entire 20th Century [Infographic]. *Forbes*, Forbes Magazine. https://www.forbes.com/sites/niallmccarthy/2014/12/05/china-used-more-concrete-in-3-years-than-the-u-s-used-in-the-entire-20th-century-infographic/

12 Prior, T., Giurco, D., Mudd, G., Mason, L., & Behrisch, J. (2012). *Resource depletion peak minerals and the implications for sustainable resource management, Global Environmental Change.* https://www.academia.edu/3632952/Resource_depletion_peak_minerals_and_the_implications_for_sustainable_resource_management

13 Beiser, V. (2017). Sand mining: The global environmental crisis you've never heard of. *The Guardian*, Guardian News and Media. Retrieved from https://www.theguardian.com/cities/2017/feb/27/sand-mining-global-environmental-crisis-never-heard

14 Forti, V., Baldé, C. P., Kuehr, R., & Bel, G. (2020) *The global E-waste monitor 2020.* http://ewastemonitor.info/

15 MDR, Exact. (2013). *Warum alte Küchengeräte aus dem Osten heute noch funktionieren.* T-Online, Lifestyle: Besser Leben. https://www.t-online.de/leben/id_62366296/warum-alte-elektrogeraete-aus-dem-osten-heute-noch-funktionieren.html

On spaceship earth there are no passengers; everybody is a member of the crew. We have moved to an age in which everybody's activities affect everybody else.

(MARSHALL MCLUHAN)[1]

CHAPTER THREE

Spaceship Earth – a closed system

Every single part of our material world is interdependent, limited and finite. But we have access to immaterial sources, too. If we strategically deployed these, we could make the finite infinitely available. How would that work?

DOI: 10.4324/9781003258674-4

On April 11, 1970, Apollo 13 (call sign: *Odyssey*) left planet Earth for the Moon. Its crew consisted of pilots Jack Swigert and Fred Haise, as well as commander James Lovell, a real veteran of space travel who had previously been part of the Apollo 8 crew. The first two days of the mission passed without a single problem; after 46 hours, the crew reported that the spacecraft was in excellent condition. The closest thing to a problem was that NASA Mission Control on the ground in Houston was starting to feel a little bored. However, shortly after that encouraging report, one of the oxygen tanks exploded, severely damaging another in the process. The Earth was 200,000 miles away. Swigert swiftly reported to Mission Control. When Houston replied, the astronauts were requested to repeat their words. It was then that Lovell formulated a historic sentence: "Houston, we've had a problem."

NASA directly called together all of its greatest minds and ordered them to come up with a solution. "Failure is not an option," they were told. Millions of Americans followed the rescue operation live on television.

Luckily, the Moon-landing process had not yet been set in motion; the Lunar Module, *Aquarius*, was still connected to the main craft. The crewmembers could therefore move from mothership *Odyssey* to *Aquarius*, and use the electricity, oxygen, and water stored there. Unfortunately, the Module's rations had been calculated to suffice for just two people – and for no longer than two days. The main challenge therefore was to enable the craft to significantly accelerate its journey back to Earth. In order to save energy, they decided to turn off as much equipment as possible, including the climate control and navigation systems. In addition, they flew Apollo 13 over the Moon as low as possible, so that when they reached its far side, the craft would be inserted into the shortest orbit possible, making maximal use of the lunar gravitational pull to return to Earth.

The maneuver succeeded but immediately gave rise to another urgent problem: since the three crewmembers were huddled together, breathing in a cramped space that had been designed to harbor no more than two men, carbon dioxide levels were rising rapidly. The air filters inside *Aquarius* simply didn't have enough capacity to filter the exhalations of

three men. There were some spare filter components stored in mothership *Odyssey*, but the square tail-ends of these filter tubes didn't fit the Module's air cylinders. The situation was turning desperate: if the team didn't come up with something very, very quickly, the astronauts would suffocate.

The NASA team in Houston thus feverishly searched for a solution, focusing their energies on designing a makeshift adapter for the filters that the crew members could easily create from materials available inside the ship. They came up with a kind of bypass, made up of *two lithium-hydroxide canisters, the cover to the Apollo 13 flight plan, two suit hoses, a roll of gray duct tape, two socks, and a bungee cord.* After some hasty tests in NASA's Manned Space Center, the design's blueprint was transmitted to the Apollo 13. The crew members managed to follow Houston's instructions and install the just invented adapter. Shortly afterward, the carbon dioxide levels started to fall and the alarm lights stopped flashing. On 17 April, the exhausted and emaciated crew members of Apollo 13 arrived safely back on Earth. Their odyssey was over.[2]

LIMITED EDITION

Apollo 13 is a classic example of a closed system: everything the crew may need during their journey is present on board, but that's literally all they will ever have to work with. Any problem that arises *has* to be solved using the resources available inside the spaceship, because, once the spacecraft has been launched, those resources cannot be supplemented. Anything that is lost, such as the oxygen tank in this case, is thus lost forever. It will never return. This kind of material finitude characterizes any closed system, providing everything within that system with the status of a 'limited edition.'

On a material level planet Earth, too, is a closed system. Astronaut Wubbo Ockels named her *Spaceship Earth* for a reason. He had seen her in space, surrounded by immeasurable darkness: her beauty, but her limits, too, and thus her vulnerability. Those limits are hard to grasp for the citizens of Spaceship Earth; we live in a world that is so rich and enormous (at least in relation to ourselves) that comparing it to a spaceship seems far-fetched, if not completely inappropriate. Still, the difference between the Earth and the *Odyssey* is just a matter of scale: the limits of the latter are clear and tangible because they are within sight; those of Planet Earth are far away – so far away, that within them we enjoy the comfortable illusion of infinity.

The difference between infinity and lots of space, however, is a crucial one. Remember Jim Carrey in *The Truman Show*? His world seemed limitless – nothing in it betrayed the fact that he was living in an enormous studio in which only a tiny part of the real world had been recreated. During his entire life up to that point, the space he needed had been equal to the space he had, which put him under that potent spell of infinity. But when he finally decides to sail off toward the horizon, he bumps into that very horizon – which turns out to be the outer wall of the studio.[3]

That's an important characteristic of large closed systems: you usually don't notice their borders until you hit them, whether figuratively or quite literally with the bow of your sailboat. In the latter case, you can at least turn around and sail back, but in the case of our planetary boundaries, there will be no way back: what is lost is lost.

ENERGY, DATA, INTELLIGENCE

Luckily for the Apollo 13 crew members, our material world does not dictate our entire story. In addition, to matter, we have two important and interacting *immaterial* sources: our intelligence and the information we use to describe our world. And in addition, we have access to another unlimited source: the eternal, rhythmic return of the Sun, which turns the finite into the infinite; an apple tree stops producing apples in winter, but come spring its branches will be heavy with fruit again – all thanks to that distant star.

Technically, solar energy is not infinite, of course, but for our purposes, we might as well say it is. The lifetime of a star like our Sun is roughly 10 billion years and the Sun has so far been providing Spaceship Earth with energy for about 4.5 billion years. That means that, if nothing unforeseen happens, the Earth will bask in sunlight for at least another 5 billion years. And more importantly: without the Sun, life on Earth would not even be possible.

We can thus state that in addition to our finite material resources, we have access to three infinite, immaterial resources: solar energy, the information we use to make sense of our world (data), and the infinite ways in which we can combine those data (intelligence). Not coincidentally, it was exactly the combination of these three infinite resources that powered Apollo 13's rescue operation. The carbon dioxide meter provided the crew members and the team in Houston with information about the air quality inside the Lunar Module; the data about carbon dioxide made the brains involved aware of the danger they found themselves in. If it hadn't been for this data/intelligence interaction, Jim Lovell, Jack Swigert and Fred Haise would have suffocated before anyone knew what was happening. Data provides us with ways of mapping limits before we reach them, enabling us to detect the urgency of matters before they've become irreversible; intelligence enables us to interpret this data and change course accordingly. And the Apollo 13 mission would never have been able to launch in the first place without energy.

Our intelligence has enabled us to become so well-informed about our world that we have been able to influence it in ways unimagined by our ancestors, changing the course of our temporary existence in myriad ways. But these data and intelligence do more than inform us about the current state of the world. They enable us to predict the distant future, too: sometimes in the form of roughly sketched scenarios, and at other times as precise calculations. A group of scientists determined 'the limits to growth' as far back as 1972 in the famous report to the Club of Rome, and suspicions that our CO_2 emissions are causing climate change have been around since the second decade of the twentieth century. We had thus already (albeit vaguely) identified the limits of Spaceship Earth nearly a century ago. Of course, our predictions are never 100% accurate; they remain guesses – however educated. Still, we can use them to alter our course, away from possible disasters, in the same way that the crew members of the *Odyssey* were steered away from their extraterrestrial fate.

One of the best things about our intelligence is that it develops partly independent of the life cycles of material resources and even our own bodies. While our skin starts sagging and our energy levels go down, our knowledge can keep growing – up to a certain point, of course. And because of our ability to exchange information, the mental abilities (whether organic or digital) of mankind can potentially grow forever.

While our physical world is characterized by its limits, our mental world is thus infinite, containing an infinite number of ways to combine and arrange finite material resources. That is what rescued the *Odyssey*: combining a finite supply of physical resources with our three infinite resources: *energy*, *data*, and *intelligence*.

Spaceship Earth is no different. Its material resources are limited, and the material arrangement we are currently using to organize our existence in most parts of the world (the linear economy) has us heading straight to the outer borders of its closed system. However, we too can use our immaterial resources to change the course of our journey – away from the unrelenting limits of our material world.

IN A CLOSED SYSTEM EVERYTHING IS EQUALLY IMPORTANT

Closed systems are not just characterized by material finitude: another typical thing about them is the fact that within the system, everything is important – simply because *anything* can affect *everything*. Every cog, no matter how tiny, is important and can cause big changes all by itself, because systems of interconnectivity rely upon complicated, crucial balances.

Every part thus contains the whole in a way, and is simultaneously dependent on every other component of the system it belongs to. As much as we like to think of ourselves as isolated beings (that coincidentally inhabit this planet), in reality, there is no such thing as isolation in Nature. Absolutely everything is related, not just here on Earth, but in the entire universe. That interconnectedness can be observed both on the macrocosmic and the microscopic end of the scale; the more you zoom either out or in, the more you'll find that our world is one huge ecosystem of interacting components. Every 'border' is thus a conceptual one. "You cannot draw a line around a volcano and say: only the particles that find themselves within this line are involved. The particles that make up our world respect such lines as little as ants respect the lines of human property rights," writes Hofstadter. Those lines exist in our minds – not in Nature.[4]

When you start seeing our earth as one big ecosystem, you will quickly realize how meaningless the hierarchical ranking in order of (perceived) importance is. Even the smallest of changes can have enormous consequences – a principle most elegantly explained by a metaphor invented by mathematician and meteorologist Edward Lorenz, who, in doing so, coined a term that significantly surpassed himself in terms of fame: *the butterfly effect*. While attempting to predict the weather, Lorenz's computer model discovered that the tiniest deviations in values could result in greatly different results. He therefore metaphorically concluded, during a lecture on the subject, that the flapping of the delicate wings of a butterfly in Brazil could result in a tornado in Texas.[5]

Something similar applies to most technologies: take away a miniscule part out of your smartphone and it will probably stop functioning. If the smartphone could function properly without it, it wouldn't be there in the first place. And in this respect, too, the analogy with spaceship *Odyssey* works: we might characterize a navigation system as significantly more important to a safe journey in space than something as mundane as a roll of gray duct tape – but the crew members of Apollo 13 might understandably disagree. No matter how little or banal, each part of a closed system can end up playing the lead role. The real value of a thing can thus be found in its relation to the whole system, not in the extent to which it can fulfill a fleeting human need, and especially not in the financial value attributed to it through the economic laws of supply and demand.

YOU CAN'T EAT MONEY

In a system in which everything is both limited and important, everything should be conserved with the same meticulousness – but that is difficult to grasp. We have a strong tendency to place things in a hierarchy of our own making, which we project onto the world around us. This order is by no means objective, or even subjectively accurate; it is wholly dependent on our focus, which, in turn, is dependent on whatever circumstances we have grown accustomed to. The more we become accustomed to the things that facilitate our existence, the more we become blind to our dependency on those things.

In our current society, we tend to attribute a lot of value to the creation of financial profit. This makes sense: within a capitalist system, the constant generation and reinvestment of profit is what causes economic growth, which, in turn, translates into tangible, material benefits. In addition, money simply cannot 'go off' or be consumed – it retains its value much better than most of the goods that contribute directly to material wealth. As Adam Smith wrote in *The Wealth of Nations*: "A country which abounds in those goods in one year, may be in great want of them the next."[6]

Within such a system, it is tempting to think of financial profit as being equal or even superior to the direct material wealth it creates and represents. But outside of those symbolic practices, money is just paper and metal – and in fact, most of it is not even that. Economists estimate that around 92% of the world's money is now digital: nothing but numbers in a computer.

When an economic crisis commences, nothing outside of the symbolic level changes. The amount of resources remains the same, as do the size of the workforce and other means of production. Still, from one year to the next, a recession can push billions of people into poverty – where they suffer very real material consequences. This makes our tendency to place money above direct material wealth understandable. It does not, however, make it accurate. "When the last tree has been cut down, the last fish caught, and the last stream poisoned, they will find out that they can't eat money," as a famous Native American saying puts it. The symbolic world we have created relies on the availability of all those material things money can be exchanged for. Financial value derives directly from those things. On its own, it has no value whatsoever.

THE HIERARCHY OF NEEDS

In 1943, the American psychologist Abraham Maslow published a hierarchical ranking of what he claimed to be the universal needs of human beings, which has become known as 'Maslow's pyramid.' According to his theory, humans will strive for the fulfillment of needs higher in the pyramid only if those below have been sufficiently satisfied.[7]

At the bottom of the pyramid, Maslow has placed our direct, physical needs: oxygen, nutrients, water – the most primary conditions for life. The next rank he reserved for the need for safety and security, the one above that for the necessity of social interaction, the fourth for our longing for appreciation and recognition, and at the pyramid's top he placed 'self-actualization.'

To use Maslow's terminology: if our primary needs at the bottom of the pyramid are permanently satisfied, without intervals of hunger and thirst or the occasional space crisis, we tend to underestimate our total dependence on these things. When the bottom of the pyramid crumbles, however, the whole construction collapses. We might currently spend most of our time striving for the accumulation of money, gadgets, the latest fashion, a bigger car, a promotion, social status, recognition and other abstract things found at the higher up in the pyramid which are centered around symbols of esteem and accomplishment, but this striving is facilitated by the crucial things at the bottom. The things that today seize the bulk of our attention rapidly lose all meaning without them.

Even as our culture and media begin to devote more attention to our planet's fast-growing problems, our capacity for ignoring these inconvenient truths seems to grow alongside it. To make matters worse, a problem like the approaching limits of our closed system plays right into several well-researched cognitive flaws in the way we think. "A distant problem that requires sacrifices now to avoid uncertain losses far in the future. This combination is exceptionally hard for us to accept," as the Israeli psychologist Daniel Kahneman explains.[8] But as much as both our tendency to place financial profit above our natural environment and our unwillingness to change can be explained, the fact remains that if we don't make any changes ourselves, they will be made for us – and we won't like them.

We can still alter our course, using the combination of immaterial resources described in this chapter. In order for that to happen, though, we need to be focused on that task. We need to start paying more attention to the fact that our material environment is finite, interconnected, and, above all: the very foundation of our existence. If we don't, these facts will soon enough start demanding our attention in much more unpleasant ways. And the most terrifying part of this story? Within a closed system, there is no such thing as 'reconstruction.' When we reach the outer limits of our closed system, there will be no way back. Our bridges will be burned.

NOTES

1 Mc Luhann, M. (Winter 1974). "On spaceship earth there are no passengers." Quote from "At the Moment of Sputnik" in *Journal of Communication*.
2 Howell, E., & Hickock, K. (2020). *Apollo 13: The moon-mission that dodged disaster*. Space.com, https://www.space.com/17250-apollo-13-facts.html
3 The Truman Show, 1998, Paramount Pictures.
4 Hofstadter, D. (2007). *I am a strange loop*. New York: Basic Books.
5 Lorenz E. (1972). "Does the flap of a butterfly's wings in Brazil set off a tornado in Texas?" *American Association for the Advancement of Science*.

6 Smith, A. (1723–1790). *The wealth of nations/Adam Smith*; Introduction by
   Robert Reich; Edited, with Notes, Marginal Summary, and Enlarged Index by
   Edwin Cannan. New York: Modern Library, 2000.
7 Maslow, A. H. (1943). "A theory of human motivation." *Psychological Review*,
   Vol. 50, No. 4, pp. 370–396.
8 Marshall, G. (2014). *Understand faulty thinking to tackle climate change.*
   New Scientist, https://www.newscientist.com/article/mg22329820-200-
   understand-faulty-thinking-to-tackle-climate-change/

A human being is a part of the whole called by us
universe, a part limited in time and space.

(ALBERT EINSTEIN)

CHAPTER FOUR

Permanent temporality

**Our existence is temporary, but our actions trigger
causal chains that will survive us for millions of years.
How could we begin to recalibrate the link between
our fleeting needs and the permanent consequences
of our decisions?**

DOI: 10.4324/9781003258674-5

The third and fourth dynasties of the ancient Egyptian Empire, which existed about 5,000 years ago, were characterized by economic prosperity and stability. The Egyptian pharaohs held a special position in their societies: they were seen as human incarnations of the gods. This superhuman role was not just important during the Pharaoh's lifetime, but also, and especially, after his death. Preparations for the Pharaoh's burial were therefore started long before he passed away. The ancient Egyptians believed the Pharaoh's existence would continue in the afterworld, so they treated their royal bodies with the utmost care. They were embalmed, mummified and then buried along with anything he might need on his journey through the underworld: jewelry, food and even furniture.

Initially, the pharaohs were laid to rest in stately tombs, carved out of stone and covered with rectangular constructions. These *mastabas* (Arabic, meaning *low bench*) were the precursors to the pyramids we still find in Egypt today. Around 2,630 BC, the first pyramid was built in Saqqara, for a Pharaoh named Djoser. His grave started out as a normal mastaba, but evolved into a much more ambitious project: a physical symbol of his eternal life, constructed by the high priest and architect Imhotep. Over the course of Djoser's reign, which lasted for nearly 20 years, a construction consisting of six layers of stone was built. Its 62 meters made it the highest man-made structure to have been built up to that time.[1]

From then on, being buried in a pyramid became the norm for a long succession of Egyptian royals, and the size and stateliness of these pyramids kept increasing. The results can still be admired at several locations in modern-day Egypt: tour buses full of tourists travel back and forth from Cairo to the pyramids every day of the year. Meanwhile, anno 2019, in some air-conditioned office building in the capital, a civil servant's day job consists of the maintenance of these final resting places.

TEMPORARY BEINGS

This story illustrates the discrepancy between the temporality of 'being' and the sheer permanence of our action's consequences.

Pharaoh Djoser's life did not last any longer than the life of an average person today. On the contrary, it was most likely a significantly shorter life, since people (even incarnated gods) usually did not live past their forties. Even so, the decisions made by this Pharaoh, 5,000 years ago, have material consequences that continue to constitute a full-time job in 2019. The causal chain set in motion by Djoser's decision has not come to an end yet, nor will it any time soon.

Our existences are temporary. Each of us will leave Spaceship Earth at some point. The atomic structures that make up our bodies today will inevitably disintegrate, and the individual atoms will go their separate ways, to form other things and other beings. Exceptions to this rule have yet to be observed. The time we spend on this planet may be increasing, but it is still characterized by inexorable finitude. In the way, that finitude is an inherent characteristic of the material resources of Spaceship Earth, temporality is an inherent characteristic of existence.

This does not just apply to our own existence. It applies equally to the existence of the laptop on which this book was written, the chair on which you might be sitting right now, and the houses we build to keep out the cold, the rain and the wind. Indeed, it applies to our entire universe: contrary to what people believed for thousands of years, our universe had a starting date. It has existed for about 14 billion years. In addition, it is likely that it will stop existing someday, either by expanding into nothingness, or by collapsing in on itself. But inasmuch as we are even aware of the temporality of our existence, and with that the temporality of our needs and wishes, we do not seem to take it into account in the way we organize our economic world. The unfathomable numbers of cell phones, DVD players, stereos, copiers, laptops, tablets, and televisions we discard each year attest to this.

As we have mentioned before, the Global E-waste Monitor 2020 found that a record 53.6 million metric tons of electronic waste was generated in 2019. Only 17.4% was officially documented as properly collected and recycled.[2] Each of these devices was produced to fulfill the temporary need of a temporary being. When either that need or that being came to an end, the devices were discarded and turned into e-waste – contributing to the global environmental problem.

Moreover, according to a study by McKinsey and the Ellen McArthur Foundation, most of these goods have lost 95% of their raw material value after only one cycle of usage. Currently, only a fraction of the resources used by our industries consists of recycled materials. In a scenario in which all valuable resources would be recycled – and the necessary precautions to preserve the value of these resources would have been taken – the amount of money saved would be staggering.[3]

The same United Nations University study found that the total value of all raw materials present in electronic waste worldwide in 2019 was approximately 57 billion euros. A harvest society is not just a good idea for our environment: it is also highly beneficial to our economies.

TEMPORARY NEEDS

It is not beyond our powers to act otherwise. Enough scenarios exist in which we demonstrate how capable we are of taking into consideration the temporary nature of our needs and wishes. The more aware we are of the impermanence of a need, the more we think about ways to facilitate its temporality – probably because, in most of these scenarios, *we're* the ones being confronted with the extended consequences of our decisions. In addition, the short, uncomplicated causal chains set into motion by those choices leave little room for doubt as to the relation between a decision and a consequence.

When we set out on a camping holiday, we leave our lounge suite, our espresso machine and that costly, 36-piece tableware set we inherited from our grandparents at home. It is easy to see why bringing these things with us would be highly impractical: their permanent (due to weight and/or immobility) Nature does not match the temporary nature of the needs that arise during a three-week camping vacation. Instead, we bring a carefully measured amount of stuff: three pairs of shorts, two sweaters, five shirts, enough underwear for a week, enough washing detergent for two laundry washes, an easy-to-set-up tent, those handy camping chairs and a set of small plastic bottles, containing just enough shampoo and shower gel for about 25 showers. In other words: we adapt our actions to the temporality of our needs. As a result, we won't end up having to leave our three-piece sofa on the campsite at the end of a trip, due to an unforeseen lack of space in the car. We simply fold up our lightweight camping chairs, which we will store on top of a big pile in the garage when we get home – where they will be waiting for us the next time the need for temporary, portable seating arises.

The way we facilitate those temporary needs develops all the time, under the influence of technology. We used to spend hours deliberating which books to bring on our beach holiday; bringing a stack of books with us to someplace where a different language is spoken, after all, was a situation in which we found ourselves in a kind of closed system, too. Once you had arrived, your books could not be supplemented. Today, however, we can simply bring a tablet or an e-reader, which provides us with access to pretty much every book we might want to read. As long as we have to deal with the consequences of our decisions ourselves, we can apparently be quite inventive when it comes to facilitating temporality. And yet, when the causal chain gets even slightly longer and more complicated – yet no less causal – we immediately dissociate ourselves from these extended consequences.

How far our idea of 'responsibility' follows the causal chain started by our decisions is a social phenomenon that differs from culture to culture. The dominant custom in most contemporary Western cultures is to cut the chain short mentally. This is not just disastrous for our environment: it's as impractical as bringing our sofa on a camping trip. Until recently, we might have been able to defend the defeatist position which holds that, due to our levels of sophistication, our self-manufactured reality has become so complicated that this custom is simply inevitable: our world is just *that* much more complicated than that of our ancient forebears – or that of Native American tribes praised for living in harmony with their surroundings. The complexity of modern civilization, according to this argument, makes it impossible to keep track of who is responsible for what: the causal chains set in motion by our decisions get so tangled up with those of others that they become indistinguishable from them. This plays into another well-known psychological fallacy: as it becomes harder to distinguish our actions from those of others, we become less inclined to work for good results. In social psychology, this phenomenon is called 'social loafing.' In recent years, however, we have reached a level of technological sophistication that not only provides the necessary transparency but renders us capable of dealing with this complexity – and untangling our individual responsibilities. Useful tools have been developed: tools that we can effectively use to get a grip on all those causal chains flowing from our every decision.

As soon as we start accepting the responsibilities resulting from those decisions, we will have an incentive to make much better decisions as individuals. We will be able to do so in two different ways, both of which exemplified by our camping holiday:

1   We can anticipate the temporality of our needs, consider for how long we will need something and act accordingly (as in the case of our fold-up camping chairs)
2   Using a combination of data and modern technology, we can turn the physically finite (a pile of books) into the immaterially infinite (millions of e-books online).

Both of these methods keep limited material resources infinitely available. And both are already widely in use: all we need to do is to scale them up.

TYPES OF TEMPORALITY

If we are going to start taking into consideration the temporary nature of our needs, we will have to distinguish between three different kinds of temporary needs. There exists the kind of temporary need characterized by a predetermined duration: needs that arise during a camping holiday, a funfair, a picnic in the park. This form of temporality is characterized by the possibility to anticipate the exact time it will take and make preparations accordingly.

Another form of temporality is one that we will refer to as 'changeable needs.' While the global need itself here remains constant, the way in which it can be fulfilled continuously undergoes little changes. Think of a child in need of a bicycle: at first, this bicycle will need to have three wheels; after a while, it must lose one of its back wheels, grow a little bigger, and it will need two little training wheels attached to its back wheel; later on still, the training wheels will need to be removed again, after which the rapidly growing child will soon need an even bigger model. The need ('bicycle') remains constant, but the precise fulfillment of that need changes constantly.

This second form of temporality applies as well if the context in which a product is used changes, either through technological innovation or societal changes. This is the type of temporality manipulated in the 'designed to be old-fashioned' and 'designed to be uncool' business models. In those models, the general needs (communication, mobility, being dressed) never actually change, but these functional needs are tied to psychological needs (staying up-to-date, maintaining a certain identity) through marketing strategies developed by industries that benefit from our constantly purchasing new goods. Hence, the products we use to fulfill our needs undergo changes faster than we could ever keep up with – leaving us always one step behind of their fulfillment.

The third kind of temporary needs (and the most common one) is characterized by two principles: (1) we know these needs are temporary, but (2) we have no clue as to how long they will be around. We know, for instance, that our lives are finite. Our need for the things we use to support and sustain ourselves – a house, furniture, clothing, kitchen supplies – will thus come to an end someday. We are equally aware of the fact that the company for which we're building a shiny new headquarters will cease to exist someday, or perhaps it will reorganize so that it needs a much smaller building, or expand to the point that it requires a building that will make the Empire State Building seem like a garden shed. Who knows? And that's the point exactly: nobody does.

A GIANT FAIRGROUND ATTRACTION

What if, each time we would go camping at our favorite campsite in the south of France, we would build and at the end of the summer leave a new house on the terrain? The house would slowly decline after our departure, the materials that went into its construction would go to waste, and the owner of the campsite would soon be encumbered with a ruin on his property. It doesn't take much imagination to see how impractical that would be. And yet, we do the exact same thing when we construct whole buildings for the purpose of fulfilling temporary needs, using finite material resources without ever giving a thought as to how to take the proverbial tent down again. This doesn't have to be: it's perfectly possible to use the same, practical form of advance planning for the construction of a building as it is for a quick-pitch tent.

A fairground attraction, for instance, has been designed in a way that makes it easy to take the whole installation apart without losing a single one of its components: every connection, every last detail of the design anticipates this temporality. If it didn't, the showman would have to buy new parts every few days, which would make it difficult to run a profitable business. He works not so much with 'real estate' as with 'mobile estate' – and we can learn a lot from him. Since every one of our needs is temporary, *all* estate should be mobile. Our buildings and products are in fact one giant fairground attraction.

All we should really distinguish between are short-term mobile estates (our quick-pitch tent) and long-term mobile estates (the Egyptian pyramids). We should never again construct a building without having anticipated, in the initial design, a way to take it apart again. If we manage to design our entire economy in this new way – one that takes

into account the temporary nature of our needs as well as the permanent consequences of our actions – we can keep the limited material resources of our closed system in the loop forever. All that is required is thinking ahead.

In our linear economic system, we indifferently discard valuable, scarce materials – knowing that we will never see them again. The guiding principle in this practice is meeting our current needs and wishes, the fleeting nature of which is entirely disproportionate to the extended nature of the consequences of these actions.

BACK TO THE FUTURE

Nobody knows what the future will look like. Our predictions will always be just that: predictions, dream scenarios that often tell us more about the time in which they were articulated than they do about the time they are prophesying about. Our fantasies about the future change all the time, after all: each new technology makes people imagine a new kind of scenario. Technological development influences societal norms, and vice versa: developments in society (whether ideological, economic, or demographic) influence the focal points of technological development. This means that even if we were able to formulate somewhat educated guesses about the technological possibilities of the future, we still could not foresee which of these possibilities would be realized – and why or how – they would influence our daily world.

On YouTube, one can find several videos from the 1950s, in which the makers have predicted what "the kitchen of the future" will look like: amazed housewives opening kitchen cabinets with just a wave of their hands, selecting meals from a screen, pushing a button here and there, and serving impressive-looking dishes the minute their husbands come home from work. The technological predictions in these videos were, if not exactly accurate, not so very far from the truth. This has not resulted in masses of amazed housewives sitting around in admiration of their futuristic household devices all day, however: it has resulted in masses of women putting all that freed-up time to use by getting a job of their own, which, in turn, has resulted in a huge shift away from traditional gender roles.[4]

Even just over 20 years ago, no one could have predicted what the world would look like today. In the late 1990s, people were asked in questionnaires whether they thought they would ever use a mobile phone. Most people stated that they didn't see why they would need one: they already had a phone at home and another at the office – if friends and family needed to talk, surely they could just reach them there? They did not see what could possibly be so pressing that it couldn't wait a few hours.

In today's world, it is considered almost rude to wait half an hour before replying to a WhatsApp message. A 2018 study conducted by the American insurance company Asurion found that, even when on a holiday, the average American checks his or her smartphone 80 times a day – with 10% of participants checking their phones 300 times a day.[5] Even though two decades ago nobody could imagine ever needing a smartphone, most people today can no longer imagine a world without smartphones. "No other technology has impacted us like the mobile phone. It's the fastest growing man-made phenomenon ever: from zero to 7.2 billion in three decades," said Kevin Kimberlin, chairman of Spencer Trask & Co. in 2014.[6]

Since 2014, there have been more cell phones than people on Earth. Experts now however predict that smartphones will only be around for another decade at most – after which they will be replaced with even 'smarter' things: things that don't have to be held or charged all the time. Facebook, Google and Microsoft are all working on developing augmented-reality headsets that project 3D-images straight onto your eyes. In a 2018 interview, Claudia Nemat, the CTO of Deutsche Telekom, predicted the end of the smartphone: "...not today, but maybe in 10 years. The smartphone will be replaced in many areas, I am convinced," she said. "Where you use the Google translator app on your smartphone in a conversation today, you'll soon find yourself using an earplug that whispers a simultaneous translation into your ear."[7]

When we zoom out and see smartphones for the very temporary phenomenon they are, the enormous environmental cost of their production becomes even more shocking. An astonishing amount of limited, rare materials, formed over the course of billions of years, has already been mined and used – for the production of devices that individually last for only a few years and as a phenomenon will only be relevant for a few decades of human history. Anything we might have wanted to do with those materials in the future has been sabotaged by our own short-sightedness.

AN OPTION WITH A FUTURE

For those who don't know the future, only one course of action makes sense: taking an 'option' on the future. We will have to rethink our actions based on a new, heightened awareness of the unknowability of the future, and the temporary nature of our needs and wishes. We will have to organize our economy in such a way that everything needed for the realization of an option – the fulfillment of a temporary need – will be released again after this particular option expires, available for the realization of new options: options on the future of the future.

Our existence on Earth is analogous with an open-ended journey: we don't know how long it will take, or what we will end up needing further down the road. All we know is that our time is finite, and this single certainty will henceforth have to lie at the heart of all our economic deliberations and motivations. Acknowledging the limitations of your own perspective is, after all, the foundation of all wisdom. "I know that I'm intelligent, because I know that I know nothing," Socrates is supposed to have said around 2,000 years ago. We would like to borrow this thought and adapt it to our message: "We know that we are preparing for the future, if we are fully aware of the fact that we cannot predict it." The very best way to ensure enduring access to whatever it is we will need, therefore is by simply keeping *everything* available. Finding a way to do this would bring our economic system in line with the main principles of both our own existence (temporality) and the resources of Planet Earth (physical finitude). "Today's products must become tomorrow's resources – for yesterday's prices," the Swiss architect and founder of the Genevan Product-Life Institute Walter Stahel famously said. He could not have been more right.

Walter Stahel is seen as the intellectual father and founder of the Circular Economy, though he himself prefers to use the term *Performance Economy*. In his 1976 report to the European Commission 'Potential for Substituting Manpower for Energy', he outlined how a system of product-life extension – through repairs and the sale of products as a service – would lead to job creation, economic competitiveness, resource savings and waste prevention.[8] He thus developed the basic features of the Circular Economy. In 1982, the report was published as a book.

During a visit to Geneva in early 2018, Walter Stahel told us about his work so far, and his vision on the economy. He emphasized the fact that the Circular Economy should be an economy of circles, what he means is that it is very important to design our products and buildings in a way that their materials can circulate in open loops through our economic system. As much as Stahel's thinking is gaining recognition and influence, it is unfortunately still far from dominating the way we design products or buildings today.

If, around the time of Stahel's European Commission report, we had started designing our products – from televisions to high-rise buildings – so that, more than just being products, they had become *resource depots*, we would now be able to 'harvest' the resources used for their production and use them for other purposes. We could then simply disassemble the billions of smartphones that were produced in the past ten years and use the resources that went into their production for new purposes – such as augmented reality headsets and translation earplugs. Of course, that would only be possible if material did not just circulate within a company but also between companies, to secure their long-term preservation.

Such an economy would make the difference between a Throwaway Society that rapidly depletes the finite resources of a closed system, and a regenerative Harvest Society in line with the fundamental principles of that closed system. Harvesting means adapting to the laws of Nature, taking care of the fertility of your fields in the future, and being conscious of the fact that you are a tiny part of something much bigger. It means being aware of the generations that will come after you and the complex physical laws that link your world to theirs. In all those respects, it is the opposite of the way we currently exploit our natural world – at the expense of its livability for ourselves, of other creatures and future generations of Earth's inhabitants.

Every year, an organization called the Global Footprint Network calculates that year's Earth Overshoot Day.[9] This is the day on which humanity has consumed all the recoverable resources available for the year as a whole. And every year this day moves closer to January. In 2022, the world had used Nature's resource budget of that year by July 28, while in 2018, it was the 1st of August. This was a worldwide average, however: the way in which these resources are divided and distributed over different countries of course is highly unequal. If everyone in the world lived like the inhabitants of the United States, in 2022, Earth Overshoot Day would have taken place as early as the 13th of March – and we would have found ourselves in need of four planet Earths. If on the other hand the entire world population lived like the population of Ecuador does, Earth Overshoot Day wouldn't have taken place until December 6. The people in the Global South consume significantly less, but will be more affected by the ecological consequences than those in the Global North.

HARVESTING IN THE ANTHROPOCENE

Far from being new or modern, the principle of harvesting resources was common until the advent of the Industrial Revolution: resources were reused all the time. Archeologists are less excited about this, since it means that a lot of old buildings have simply disappeared: taken apart so that their materials could be used for the construction of new houses or temples, sometimes even pulverized into cement. Most of the swords that fought ancient wars have long since been melted down and turned into something else.

The difference between these civilizations and ours, however, is that – due to technological advancement – we have started creating complex products and new, often toxic materials whose chemical components cannot just be taken apart again or be re-melted. In 2008, the Royal Geological Society in London officially acknowledged that the Earth has entered a new geological age: the Anthropocene, the human age, characterized by man's immense influence on the Earth's atmospheric, biological and geological processes – resulting in climate change, pollution, species extinction and resource waste.[10] If this age is ever interpreted by future geologists, based on the remains of the materials that characterize our world, these materials will be aluminum, plastic, and concrete.

The Anthropocene has been officially recognized since 2008, but the consequences of this age of human domination and its linear economy have been an important subject in politics and society at least since the publication of the Brundtland report (titled 'Our Common Future') in 1987, or the Earth Summit in Rio de Janeiro in 1992.[11] Since then, numerous scientists have developed models that have predicted the inevitable material shortages and the ecological consequences of the Anthropocene. Adequately praising everyone who has worked towards getting these subjects on the agenda would take a book of its own, but we would still like to highlight a few that we were lucky enough to meet in person through our work and who have inspired us particularly. Interestingly enough we met most of them after having pioneered sustainable and circular concepts for some decades ourselves and discovered that there were others in quest of the same answers.

In addition to Walter Stahel, whom we already mentioned, there have been numerous other schools of thought and thinkers that have served as important pioneers of the circular economy. For decades, the chemist Michael Braungart and the architect William McDonough have concerned themselves with the question of how to produce products – in terms of design and chemical makeup – in such a way that they can be recycled without harming humans or the environment. Their approach can be summed up by one principle: waste is food. The pair proposed that after products reach the end of their useful life, they should become either 'biological nutrients' or 'technical nutrients.' Biological nutrients are materials that can re-enter the environment, while technical nutrients are materials that remain within closed-loop industrial cycles. Braungart and McDonough call this approach Cradle to Cradle (as opposed to Cradle to Grave, which is how the linear economy is often described). Consequently, it is very important to avoid toxic substances. Braungart's biggest concern about the Circular Economy is that it could keep substances that are harmful to humans and the environment in perpetual material cycles.[12]

What fascinates us particularly about Cradle to Cradle in a practical sense is the cross-sectoral network, which emerged inspired by Cradle to Cradle. Since its design principles are relevant and applicable to almost every sector, Cradle to Cradle brings together a great variety of different actors, all from completely different disciplines. The movement has facilitated collaborations between companies and individuals who, when they started, had no idea of how much they could benefit from this exchange. It has laid the foundation for an awareness of the complexity of today's problems – and the realization that a one-dimensional answer will always remain inadequate. This cross-sectoral awareness has been the first, indispensable step towards finding a truly holistic answer.

Another important inspiration to us has been the American biologist and founder of Biomimicry, Janine Benyus. Benyus has pioneered groundbreaking insights into Nature's design principles, in order to make them applicable to industrial processes. Her core idea is that Nature has already solved many of the problems we are facing today – and that we should perceive our surroundings as a giant library of learning. As the British architect Michael Pawlyn puts it: "You could look at nature as being like a catalog of products, and all of those have benefited from a 3.8 billion year research and development period. Given that level of investment, it makes sense to use it."[13]

The Wuppertal Institute for Climate, Environment and Energy in Germany has played an important role in changing the way economists, policy makers and business leaders think about wealth creation. The research institute began work in 1991, under the German scientist and politician Ernst Ulrich von Weizsäcker.[14] The institute explores resource, climate and energy challenges in their interactions with society and the economy. Von Weizsäckers has published two books based on the institute's findings, which demonstrate how technical innovation can drastically increase resource productivity, decoupling economic prosperity from resource consumption.

Despite all these remarkable efforts, and despite the immense wealth of knowledge in this realm that has accumulated over the past decades, real awareness of the need for fundamental change has yet to pervade our businesses and society at large.

Yes, sustainability became a trending topic in the forms of the Global Reporting Initiative, the Dow Jones Sustainability Index and the like, but more as a checklist of hygiene factors than a core principle on which to build the economy. John Elkington, another sustainability pioneer whom we highly value, 25 years ago famously coined the triple-bottom line as a management framework to examine a company's social, environmental and economic impact. The framework was widely adopted by leading corporations worldwide and led to the above-mentioned new ways of reporting. In 2018, however, Elkington publicly recalled his framework in the *Harvard Business Review* – arguing that it never was intended to be a checklist for accountants, but rather an instrument for system change. He calls for 'radical intent' which will stop us from overshooting our planetary boundaries and for "a new genetic code for tomorrow's capitalism: a triple helix for value creation, spurring the regeneration of our economies, societies, and biosphere … We must change hearts and minds, including our own."[15]

The Fridays for Future movement is a first sign that the needle might tip into the right direction, but radical action is needed and fast. Regardless of the fact that nearly every stock-listed company has a chief sustainability officer, sustainability is still widely seen as the antithesis to cost-effectiveness – rather than seeing these two concepts as being largely synonymous. This has unnecessarily split the social field: companies versus environmental activists, the ministry of economics versus the ministry of environment, hippies versus yuppies. The result is a society in which little has happened over the past decades, while we have kept on rushing towards the limits of our closed system.

However in the past few years we are starting to see some signs of change, which make us hopeful – mainly due to the term 'Circular Economy.' Although this change is not driven by a change of hearts and minds, more and more companies seem to be beginning to see the enormous economic potential of a sustainable, resource-efficient model. At the same time, the financial sector has slowly started to comprehend the risks arising from our impending resource scarcity.

The breakthrough of this thinking is primarily the merit of British sailor and activist Ellen MacArthur. Her foundation was the first to initiate a report calculating the enormous potential of the circular economy, and to prove its feasibility on the basis of case studies. The report, put together by management consulting firm McKinsey, was published in 2012. Since then, the Ellen MacArthur foundation has brought together numerous major alliances of companies, organizations and scientific and government institutions dedicated to the understanding and implementation of the circular economy.[16] We enjoyed the honor of being present at the very first presentation of this report, having created one of the first working examples of the circular economy, as we will describe in Chapter 5.

RE-MELTING OUR SWORDS

Due to the earlier described chemical complexity – and often toxic nature – of the materials that dominate the Anthropocene, we can no longer simply re-melt our sword or pulverize our building in order to use it as the cement of the future. Instead, we have to *think ahead*.

We now have the technological sophistication to run such an operation of planning ahead – but the workings of a society are determined by more than technological sophistication alone; otherwise, planned obsolescence would not have existed in the first place. The question is: how to get a firm enough grip on our complex social and economic world to realize this idea of a Harvest Society.

In their current form, government regulations are not effective enough. History, meanwhile, has shown us how dangerous it can be to give governments the amount of unchecked power needed to effectively make such changes – so this is not something we recommend either. Given the powerlessness of consumers, as described in the first two chapters, it would be equally imprudent to put them in charge of changing the world. The answer is, we need all actors in the economic arena: governments, consumers and the private sector. The producers of most of the goods in our economic system have a crucial role to play in realigning their core activities with the boundaries of the planetary system. But the aim of private companies is to make a profit for their stockholders, not to work for the collective good or the health of our planet. Should we convince private actors to do the world a favor and abandon their self-interest? "Rather than counting on people's readiness to do you a favor, simply trust that they won't make any decisions that conflict with their self-interest," the Italian political philosopher Machiavelli famously advised his readers in the sixteenth century – and we agree.[17] We therefore propose not to rely on the readiness of private companies to abandon their self-interest, but to do the opposite: to rely on their readiness and capability to act in their own interest. After all, it is these exact qualities that make a company successful.

What if there were a way to bring the preservation of resources in agreement with the self-interest of producers? Of making producers financially responsible for the environmental consequences of their own decisions? Not as an afterthought, but from the very start of our chain of production – and all the way down to the end of the line.

Our assertion is that instead of our current Throwaway Society we need to build a Harvest Society in which the financial interests of manufacturers would fall into agreement with the boundaries of our planetary system. How do we get there? Simply by changing the rules of the game.

NOTES

1 Mark, J. J. (2016). The step pyramid of Djoser. *Ancient History Encyclopedia*, Ancient History Encyclopedia. Retrieved from www.ancient. eu/article/862/the-step-pyramid-of-djoser/

2 Forti, V., Baldé, C. P., Kuehr, R., & Bel, G. (2020). *The global E-waste monitor 2020.* http://ewastemonitor.info/

3 Ellen MacArthur Foundation (2015). *Growth within: A circular economy vision for a competitive Europe.* https://www.ellenmacarthurfoundation.org/ assets/downloads/publications/EllenMacArthurFoundation_Growth-Within_ July15.pdf

4 Nepley (2008). *Kitchens of the future.* https://www.youtube. com/watch?v=TiACOLuYlJ4&t=185s

5 Asurion (2019). *Americans aren't taking a break from their phones.* https:// www.asurion.com/connect/tech-tips/americans-arent-taking-a-break- from-their-phones

6 Page, C. (2014). *There are now more active mobile devices than humans.* The INQUIRER. https://www.theinquirer.net/inquirer/news/2374525/there-are- now-more-active-mobile-devices-than-humans

7 "Telekom-Vorstand Claudia Nemat Im Interview." (2018). *Teachtoday*, Helliwood Media & Education. https://www.teachtoday. de/Informieren/Digitale_Kommunikation/2575_Claudia_Nemat_im_ Interview.htm

8 Reday-Mulvey, G., Stahel, W. R., & Commission of the European Communities. (1977). *The potential for substituting manpower for energy: Final report 30 July 1977 for the Commission of the European Communities.* Geneva, Switzerland: Battelle, Geneva Research Centre.

9 Earth Overshoot Day, *Footprint Network.* https://www.footprintnetwork. org/our-work/earth-overshoot-day/

10 Members of the Stratigraphy Commission of the Geological Society of London (2008). The Anthropocene Epoch: Today's Context for Governance and Public Policy. The Geological Society, The Geological Society of London. Retrieved from https://www.geolsoc.org.uk/Geoscientist/Letters/2008/The- Anthropocene-Epoch-todays-context-for-governance-and-public-policy

11 World Commission on Environment and Development (1987). *Our common future.* Oxford: Oxford University Press.

12 McDonough, W., & Braungart, M. (2009). *Cradle to cradle: Remaking the way we make things.* London: Vintage.

13 "What Is Biomimicry?" *Biomimicry Institute.* Website: https://biomimicry. org/what-is-biomimicry/

14 *Wuppertal Institut Für Klima, Umwelt, Energie.* Website: https://wupperinst. org/en

15 Elkington, J. 25 Years ago I coined the phrase 'Triple Bottom Line.' Here's why it's time to rethink it. *Harvard Business Review*, 13 September. 2018. https:// hbr.org/2018/06/25-years-ago-i-coined-the-phrase-triple-bottom-line-heres- why-im-giving-up-on-it

16 Ellen MacArthur Foundation (2012). *Towards the circular economy.* Report Volume 1. London: Ellen MacArthur Foundation.

17 Machiavelli, N., & Wootton, D. (1995). *The prince.* Indianapolis, IN: Hackett Pub. Co.

Every right implies a responsibility; every opportunity an obligation; every possession a duty.

(JOHN D. ROCKEFELLER)

CHAPTER FIVE

Changing the rules of the game

More and more products are being offered as a service. We drive cars that aren't ours, make holiday in someone else's home and access extensive music libraries without owning a single album. Still, these developments do not change the nature of the linear economy. Why not? And which rules are necessary for actual change?

DOI: 10.4324/9781003258674-6

In the spring of 2010, we decided to restyle our office in East Amsterdam; after about 20 years, RAU Architects was in need of a makeover. We asked Philips to design a plan regarding the lighting of the newly furnished space. The day before the Philips people arrived, I was looking out of one of our office windows when I noticed a pile of discarded heaters the building bordering ours was apparently awaiting new owners. The gloomy sight of those 40 or 50 heaters declared obsolete put me in a strange, melancholy mood. Ever since we had been one of the first enterprises to open an office in Amsterdam's eastern docklands, we had seen basically every building in the area being built or renovated. How is it possible, I thought to myself, that I have been here longer than the time it takes for a heater to be discarded?

The thought stuck in my mind. The next day, when Philips sales manager Erik Heutink – a man we will not soon forget – rang our doorbell, I asked him to come in, but to leave his lamps in the car: I had a proposition for him. "Look," I explained. "I want first-rate lighting, which is why I contacted your company, but I've decided that I don't want to own your lamps. I just want to use their light." The man stared at me with a blank look on his face.

I tried again.

> Your usual plan boils down to installing all kinds of splendid lamps that, from then on, will provide our office with the light which we need to work after sundown. Philips then sends me a bill, I pay, and the lamps become my property. That's how this usually works – but I want something different. I'm not interested in the product itself, I'm interested in what it produces: 300 lux, about 2,000 hours a year. Just how Philips makes that happen isn't really my concern.

Confused, the salesman said he would have to talk this over with his boss – he would get back to me. But then, half an hour after he had left, he called me up from his car.

> Mr. Rau, I don't think I fully comprehend your plan, but I'm interested enough to give it a chance. I will accept your request – even though I have no clue as to where this will lead us. I have one condition, though: we're not yet telling my boss.

He came back a few weeks later, bringing along a light consultant and an elaborate lighting plan listing all the lamps we would need for the amount of illumination we had requested. I thanked them kindly.

"Just one more thing," I said.

> The electricity bill is, of course, yours. Your lamp doesn't work without electricity. That happens to be the way you've designed it. All I have ordered is *light*, though. If you need electricity for that, that is your concern – not mine. If you can produce lamps that run on red or white wine, I'll happily take those.

The sales manager was visibly taken aback. "Well, that changes things a little bit," he concluded nervously, after a long silence. The designers would have to go through the lighting plan again, he explained, and he would come back with a new proposition afterward.

Together with Heutink's team and Robert Metzke, today Philips Global Head Sustainability and at that time responsible for Philips' Ecovision program, we developed a holistic concept. When finished, the plan was unrecognizable. Apparently, the same kind of lighting could actually be achieved with far fewer lamps – and that wasn't the only thing that had changed: the designers had come up with all kinds of technical solutions that reduced the power consumption to an absolute minimum. After all, Philips would have to pay that bill.

That is how RAU Architects became the first-ever user of light as a service – which decreased our energy consumption by 44%. A new business model was born. Today, Philips Lighting now called Signify promotes it all over the world, rebranded as Circular Lighting.

PRODUCT AS A SERVICE

Even though we never could have predicted the scope of the impact generated by our plan, we did, of course, anticipate the situation our new rules would produce. Under the old rules, more lamps automatically meant more revenue for Philips, but in the new situation, Philips increased their revenue by providing us with *fewer* lamps. In addition, it was in the best interests of the company to manufacture lamps that would last as long as possible. After all, if the lights needed replacement, repair, or maintenance, Philips would be paying the bill.

The sales manager found himself in an unprecedented situation: he was suddenly confronted by one problem after another – problems originally meant for consumers were now boomeranging back to his company.

Consequently, our office wasn't filled with energy-guzzling halogen lamps, TLs, or bulbs. When the Philips people finally came to install the new lighting plan, we witnessed how the finest, modularly designed, low-energy LED lamps were installed in our office – lamps we never could have afforded if had we bought them ourselves under the traditional model. Suddenly, we were equipped with the best lighting available on the market. And the longer they lasted, the more revenue Philips made. Win-win.

We started approaching other companies, too, motivated by this success. The 1,000 square meters of our office became one big, experimental playground – under the slogan *practice what you preach*. We bought 'walking' hours from carpet manufacturers Interface and Desso, and 'sitting' and 'table' hours from Steelcase.

It usually took a little while for producers to understand the meaning of this new model; almost everyone initially tried to get away with a green-seeming lease contract. Eventually, however, we made the same deal with everyone: when the contract term ended, the lamps, carpets, desks, and chairs were returned to the manufacturer.

It was a great success: we understood that we were on to something. We had spent 20 years trying to convince the construction sector of the importance of thinking ahead, to remain viable as well as for the reasons explained in the previous chapters. Suddenly we seemed to have found the key: a new business model, based on *use* instead of *ownership* – shifting the responsibility for products back to the people making decisions about the way they are manufactured. The best thing was:

producers were enthusiastic, too. Many companies asked us to develop and launch this model with them. We decided our model was in need of a name. On October 10, 2010, *Turntoo* was founded.[1]

USE BUT NOT OWN

Using a product without owning it is not a new concept in and of itself. It's the way many of us acquire a place to live or work, and the way we often use cars, bikes, holiday homes, tuxedos, and tools. Sometimes because we only wish to use the product temporarily, and at other times, because we cannot afford (or simply do not want) to purchase the item.

In the world of business especially, the equipment we use, from the crane lorry and the passenger car to the PC and the printer, seldom belongs to the company we work for. This is called 'renting' or 'leasing' – two existing business models based on using products without owning them. Unfortunately, however, these models don't lead to the results described above. Why not? Because they don't address the problematic gap between *power* and *responsibility.*

Leasing is simply a financial model that was invented after World War II. It was introduced to stimulate consumption in an economy in which people didn't have enough money to purchase products as expensive as, say, cars.

Today, an entire industry revolves around clever enticements designed to tempt the customer to consume more than he or she can currently afford. During a lease contract term, however, the *bank* becomes the legal owner of the product – not the producer. Ownership thus shifts from the producer to the financial institution, still separating power and responsibility. A financial institution, after all, has just as little influence on the manufacturing process as a consumer does.

The rules by which leasing arrangements are governed therefore don't alter the linear nature of the economy – on the contrary: they speed up its negative effects, as they encourage people to consume without financial restrictions.

Renting is a different story, too. Consumers do not (usually) enter into a rental agreement with the producer of the goods that are being rented out: they are renting from people who have already purchased the product from the manufacturer. We rent a car from Hertz – not Chrysler or GM. If we want to cycle around for a day, we contact a local bike rental company, not the bike factory. A rental agreement, too, therefore separates power and responsibility.

Of course: a rental company does experience stronger incentives than the average consumer to buy strong, durable products that are in need of little maintenance, but even this incentive is really just another optimization of the linear economy – and thus by no means a solution to its problems.

THE UBERFICATION OF EVERYTHING

Purchasing a service instead of a product is not a new phenomenon, either. Anyone who uses public transport does so on a daily basis. Who would want to purchase an entire Boeing 747 when planning a trip to Singapore or New York? Train, bus and airplane tickets are nothing but short-lived service contracts, and the price of these contracts always includes the energy bill – no one ever seems to be surprised by that.

Furthermore, we borrow books from the library, listen to music through Spotify, watch programs on Netflix and cycle around big cities on bikes borrowed from docking stations. All of these constructions are service contracts, existing forms of product-as-a-service. The needs these services aim to satisfy are so changeable and/or temporary that it simply is not worthwhile to invest in owning the product itself.

Additionally, even a lot of products that traditionally *were* owned by consumers are nowadays increasingly offered as a service, many of them subscription based, a development also referred to as servitization. People in their twenties and thirties, especially, seem to be interested in ownership less and less, most likely motivated by the insecurities that characterize today's 'flexible' economy. While people used to be able to envision their futures in the form of a straightforward and predictable linear narrative, nowadays they do not have the benefit of that sense of security. Our society is changing faster than social commentators can keep up with, and our work is more and more organized in the form of projects rather than linear paths.

Most people now live their lives in the knowledge that everything they rely on could very well change overnight. This affects the way we live, talk, buy and travel. Our current job might not exist in five years – and our children might end up in professions of which nobody has even heard of yet. Therefore, while the demand for the use of cars and houses has not decreased, the willingness and/or ability to take care of the responsibilities that come with owning these things has decreased significantly. More and more, people prefer freedom and choice. *Flex* is the ultimate buzzword of our time.

Companies increasingly play into this development either by enabling temporary forms of possessing a product or by selling access to it via peer to peer sharing platforms. While MyWheels and SnappCar allow you to drive someone else's car, AirBnB arranges your temporary stay in a house or apartment you will never own, the UK-based platform HURR gives you access to the wardrobe of others and the list of sharing services is growing every day. A large-scale shift away from the sale of products and toward sharing services is thus taking place already – a development usually referred to as *the Sharing Economy* or *the Uberfication of Everything.*

Even though the Sharing Economy was hailed as being radically resource-efficient, there is no guarantee it will be. The success of AirBnB caused housing prices to soar in cities like New York, Amsterdam or Paris, forcing municipalities to enforce strict rules on renting out private space via the platform. According to a report by Schaller Consulting Raide-Hailing, services like Uber and Lynx rather increased traffic and congestion in large US cities instead of reducing it.[2]

More importantly sharing does not change the way products are being manufactured – only the way they are being sold. So while this development is proof of a growing demand for services rather than products, the sharing economy in effect still constitutes an 'optimization' of the linear economy. In fact, we believe this is one of the biggest misunderstandings about circularity: that the separation of *ownership* from *use* is enough to make something circular. We come across many leasing and sharing business models that boast the circularity label, while what they really represent is not a circle but an extended line. That is exactly why we keep stressing the importance of taking a more comprehensive perspective, of ridding ourselves of the one-dimensional tunnel vision of our current economic logic.

USE, DON'T CONSUME

What, then would be a key that opens the door to a new economy, rather than some other well-intended slogan or initiative that ends up optimizing the linear model we are currently stuck with?

We need to reunite power and responsibility, and make sure they can never be separated again – not even temporarily. Rather than a one-dimensional answer within the confines of our existing economic architecture, the innovation we need is that the suppliers of services are inseparably linked to, and accountable for, the consequences of their own actions.

If products become a service and manufacturers retain the ownership, they automatically regard each product as an investment in the future: the kind of 'option on the future' we have described in the previous chapter. It will be in their immediate self-interest to make good, sustainable products and to reduce the energy and repair bills to the absolute minimum.

In addition, they will experience strong incentives to design their goods in a manner that makes it easy to take them apart again after use – so that either the individual components or the materials that went into the production of the goods can be reused in a new product cycle. Products will thus start playing a dual role: they will facilitate a consumer's temporary needs, as well as act as material depots for producers – for whom it will become in his own best interest to save every last resource or material from being lost, as that would be detrimental to the company's bottom line.

This wealth destruction exists today, too: it has just been collectivized and detached from financial consequences for manufacturers. It's an inherent part of our linear system, in the form of the garbage pile at the end of the linear chain. Our new model in effect *privatizes* the destruction of wealth, for the benefit of basically everyone: consumers, the environment, and even the manufacturers themselves, as service contracts don't lead to one-off transactions: they establish long-term customer relations and a continuous cash flow. Through this business model, producers can decrease their dependency on increasingly fluctuating resource market prices – limiting risk and increasing stability.

Consumers can currently do no more than two things with their used-up products: they can throw them away or pass them on to other consumers. Whichever option they choose, the product will eventually end up as waste. The only difference between the two scenarios is the time it takes for the product to get to the waste-yard.

Leasing or renting does nothing to change that outcome. A brand-new car ends up at a used vehicle retailer after it has been leased or rented out for about five years. In the best-case scenario, it will enjoy a third life in Mexico or Eastern Europe before it is shipped even further South, where it will get used up and dismantled. Even then, the waste-yard awaits it in the end. The difference, again, is a matter of time.

The model proposed changes all of this. Products will move back and forth between consumers and suppliers, creating actual circles rather than extended lines. Our model therefore has the potential to eliminate waste entirely. Instead of shifting away from power via the many links of the linear chain, ownership will remain with those who can take responsibility for it. Responsibility and power will therefore stay together– and the interests of manufacturers, consumers and the environment suddenly fall into agreement.

Take, make and waste? Install, use and recreate.

DESIGNED TO PERFORM

When we implement the rules of the new model, the logic dictating our current economic world will be turned upside down, its rules inverted. Take the *Designed to Fail* business model: the technological manipulation of devices we want to use for a long time, such as washing machines, blenders or printers. It is currently in the direct interest of producers for products to break down sometime in the foreseeable future (so that consumers come back for a new item), but in the new model, it will be in the direct interest of producers for products to last as long as is technologically possible. While it is currently in the interest of producers to make sure repairing products is complicated and costly, in the new model, it will be in their interest to make sure repairs are simple, quick, and cheap.

In short: the higher the quality of a product, the more money its producer will make. In addition, to maximize their revenues, producers will need their products to be low in energy consumption and require little to no maintenance – the exact things, which both consumers and our environment so desperately need.

As manufacturers retain ownership of their products, they will additionally experience strong incentives to design their goods so that they can be taken apart entirely without losing any materials or components. That way, they will not receive useless waste, but packages of components and resources that may not be valuable in their current composition, but the individual parts of which can be 'harvested' and used for the production of new valuable goods. Products will no longer be organized problems; they will be organized material depots. *Designed to Fail* will become *Designed to Perform*.

In 2012, an Amsterdam-based housing corporation asked Turntoo for assistance while putting into practice their ambitions to decrease their CO_2 emissions and help their tenants save energy. The corporation had noticed that more and more tenants in the social segment were experiencing financial troubles because of their sky-high energy costs.

To prevent their homes from losing gas, water and light, the tenants would often prioritize paying their energy bills over paying their rent – which, of course, caused problems for the housing corporation: both its financial position and its social responsibility were at stake.

The reason for these sky-high energy bills, we found, was simple: people with little money at their disposal were being forced to buy cheap household devices – appliances that, due to low quality, tend to consume huge amounts of energy. The purchase price of these products was low, but, through their energy bills, consumers actually ended up paying a price higher than the purchase price of expensive, low-energy devices.

To put a stop to this situation, we turned to Bosch Siemens Home Appliances (B/S/H), a leading manufacturer of home appliances and made them a proposition. After some talks, we arranged for the tenants to purchase the services of low-energy fridges and washing machines for €10 a month. The offer appeared on the housing corporation's website one summer night, and a few weeks later, all 150 devices had found a new home – but, bear in mind: no new owner. The appliances remained the property and responsibility of the manufacturer.

Since this was just a pilot program, the energy bill was still addressed to the consumer, but as an example, it shows the potential of changing the rules of the game: thanks to the low-energy devices, tenants saved an average of about 300–400 euros annually, and they no longer needed financial buffers for repair or replacement costs. And not only had their financial situation improved significantly: they also reported greater enjoyment resulting from the positive experience of contributing to a livable environment. In 2018, B/S/H launched this product-as-a-service-proposition for washing machines in the Netherlands under the name Blue Movement.[3]

Digitization and the Internet of Things will play a decisive role in the development of product-as-a service-models. According to Christoph Wendker, vice president Corporate Sustainability and Regulatory Affairs at Miele, a German manufacturer of high-end domestic appliances, monitoring the use and performance of equipment will enable

manufacturers to identify potential damages due to wear and tear at an early stage and make replacements before equipment is being damaged. This again shows how important it is to link power and responsibility. If the user detects or can detect defects in a device, the damage caused is usually considerably greater than if a defective component had been replaced prematurely.

Stefan Verhoeven, CEO of Miele Netherlands, also sees the possibility of supporting users in the sustainable operation of their devices and making the devices more intelligent and thus more relevant, i.e., usable, over time through online upgrades.

DESIGNED TO BE UPDATED

The second business model that will be turned inside out is the *Designed to be Outdated* business model – the functional manipulation of products in sectors characterized by a lot of 'innovation' opportunity. Since it will be in the direct interest of producers to keep products in the possession of consumers for as long as possible, the suppliers will be incentivized to design those products in ways that make it easy to update them, instead of having to exchange them for newer models – which calls for the carefully thought-out modular construction of products. The unpredictability of the future will thus start playing a large role in the design process, as our experiences during our second project with Philips confirmed.

After the success of our first experiment, Philips' CEO was so interested in our ideas that he asked us to collaborate with his company in order to further develop the model. Around the same time, Schiphol Airport had heard about the concept and came to us for advice regarding the lighting of their 9,000-square-meter 'Lounge 2.' We decided to kill two birds with one stone.

Investment cycles at Schiphol airport have a term of around 15 years. When this term ends, an accommodation, product, or process is considered outdated and ready to be replaced. The airport's options on the future are thus always limited to 15 years. The power consumption of lights at airports is enormous, however. In many places (the departure and arrival lounges, the airstrips, in tunnels and hangars), lights remain on 24x7.

The life span of a LED light, at the time of this project, was around 50,000 hours, or about six years. Within the framework of Schiphol's investment rules, this meant that the lights would have to be installed three times in the 15-year cycle, leaving three years of unused hours of light in the end: pure wealth destruction. The principles of the Product as a Service model, however, enabled the airport to order precisely 15 years of light – based on a service contract. Philips and their partners committed themselves to the management, maintenance and innovation of the lights, retaining ownership of the entire light installation.

In order to prevent reinstalling the equipment three times, they designed a new fixture especially for this project: one that lasted for 15 years instead of six. The main reason for this impressive life span extension was another bewilderingly simple one: a tiny, yet indispensable part of its electronics had been relocated, so that it was easy to access. The built-in and difficult-to-reach 'driver' had been the LED lights' weak spot: once it broke, the entire lamp had to be replaced. Now that the driver was in the front of the lamp, it was easy to repair – without even having to take the light apart. In addition, software was installed to keep track of the need for (preventive) maintenance of individual lights, further extending the life span of the hardware and keeping the maintenance costs low. *Designed to be Outdated* had become *Designed to be Updated.*

This is just one example of the many technological possibilities that exist with regard to extending the performance cycle of products. Other kinds of *Designed to be Updated*, for instance, can relate to adjustments to the appearance of products – catering to the changeable needs of consumers.

Through modular construction, the performance cycle of products can be extended simply by purchasing a new component, rather than an entirely new device. In that way, too, the performance-based model incentivizes

producers to take into account the changeability and unpredictability of our needs while designing their products.

Hardware will be regarded as software – and our technological insights will be channeled into bringing about *real* innovations rather than superficial ones meant to tempt consumers into purchasing the latest model. Engineers and designers can stop organizing *problems* and focus their undivided attention on a much nobler project: finding *solutions.*

PRELOVED AND VINTAGE

Another way to keep innovation-sensitive products (or the materials they are made of) in the loop is by increasing the *number* rather than the *duration* of life cycles – continuously passing products on to the next segment of users. After all, products aren't the only things that come in all shapes and sizes: users do, too.

In 1962, the American communications expert Everett Rogers published a book titled *The Diffusion of Innovation.* While a certain kind of user always wanted the latest novelty, Rogers had found, another kind was satisfied with the second-newest model, and a lot of other people were perfectly happy with even older versions. He mapped five different kinds of users: *innovators, early adopters, early majority, late majority* and *laggards.*[4]

Even though they obviously weren't around yet in the 1960s, smartphones provide a good way to illustrate how Roger's theory could be applied to a circular model. Today, most 'old' smartphones end up in the drawers of *early adopter* kitchens, while in the model we are proposing, producers would be able to pass these devices (that usually still work perfectly) on to the next segment, all the way down to the *laggards* – after which cycle they can simply be taken apart, their separate components functioning as the building blocks for a new generation of products. This happens already, albeit on a small scale, to products marketed as 'refurbished.' Recent market studies have discovered a huge, largely untapped market for this kind of product. Users have indicated that in some segments, refurbished products have a better price-quality ratio than brand-new products.

Moreover, an increasing number of people today identify with the notion that *used* is not necessarily inferior to *new*. Terms like 'preloved' and 'vintage' are signposts of an upcoming lifestyle and underlying philosophy that actually favors the used over the new, on grounds as far apart as environmentalism, romanticism and/or creativity. However, today's manufacturers seldom cater to this market themselves: they leave this proposition to so-called gap-exploiter companies. Afraid of cannibalizing their own 'new' products, they miss out on the tremendous business opportunity inherent in this model.

DESIGNED FOR PASSION

In the first chapter, we also talked about the *Designed to Go out of Fashion* business model, which relies on mental manipulation to stimulate the continuous demand for new products, via the creation of fashion and trends. We described how, since the 1930s, our culture has fallen under the spell of the idea that who we are can be inferred from what we own and what we wear.

The kinds of psychological manipulation used to feed and maintain this idea, however, might very well change under the influence of the rules of the new model. After all, these methods constitute ways to tempt consumers to continuously purchase new things. If it ceases to be in the interest of producers to keep people focused on *new* and *ownership*, this will most likely be reflected in the realm of marketing. Given the enormous power of marketing and media over our mental lives (a power that is still increasing under the influence of the combined forces of nudging, Big Data, and sophisticated algorithms), this shift will probably affect the way we think. If the advertisements surrounding us focus less on *new* and *ownership*, we most likely will, too. Of course this doesn't put an end to consumption for the purpose of displaying status (as nothing probably ever will), but it might shift our focus away from quantity towards quality, and from identifying with the stuff we own to identifying with the things we do.

We already largely live in an *experience economy*. We call an Uber to take us back to our AirBnB apartment after a night out in a different city. There is a tendency toward collecting memories and photos, rather than country homes and cars, and trendsetters wear vintage clothing, organize clothing-trade parties with friends, and prefer the experience of an antique shop or a flea market to the crowds at IKEA.

These phenomena are signs of the rise of a new mentality and changing needs, even though they themselves don't constitute a long-term solution to the problem of the linear economy. The real transformation will not happen as long as the current business models prevail. The switch from selling products to selling services and retaining ownership and responsibility at the side of manufacturers would support this new mentality in a fundamental way, offering it a chance to grow into the mainstream cultural transformation.

We think that two basic notions will be especially important in bringing about a change in our behavior. The first is that enjoyment does not necessarily correlate with ownership, and the second is that used is just as good as new. Eventually, these notions might free up space in our minds and priorities for the things that actually make us happy: genuinely enriching experiences, pursuing our passions, and enjoying meaningful relationships with the people around us.

In addition, becoming more aware of temporality in general might also result in a heightened awareness of the temporality of our own lives, making us value our time more, and stimulating us to go after the things we really want – instead of escaping back into safe routines, numbed by the rush we get from consumption. Meanwhile, products will go back to playing the role they initially played: as the tools we need in order to realize our dreams and plans – rather than being the content of those dreams and plans. *Designed to Go Out of fashion* will turn into *Designed for Passion*.

A great example of what can happen if this model is adopted in the fashion industry is the denim-label Mud Jeans. In 2013, its founder Bert van Son set up an unconventional fashion company, inspired by Turntoo. Clients of Mud Jeans buy the right to wear the jeans, and after wearing them for a period of time, they return their trousers to Mud Jeans, where the denim is recycled into new pair of jeans. Forty percent of a pair of Mud Jeans is made from recycled garment already.[5]

Since last summer, Mud Jeans has even teamed up with IKEA, producing a sofa cover made of 40% post-consumer recycled denim for their famous Klippan sofa. "The KLIPPAN sofa is an iconic IKEA product. By offering new sofa covers made from recycled materials, we can help customers to renew their sofa and reuse materials," said Piotr Jakubiak, deployment leader at IKEA.[6]

Another inspiring example of a company taking long-term responsibility is Patagonia, a US-based company providing outdoor equipment and gear. For decades, Patagonia has been focusing on environmentally responsible design and production. Since as far back as 1996, all of its cotton has been sourced from organic origins. But Patagonia is always taking the next step: they attracted a lot of attention in 2011 by placing ads stating 'Don't buy this Jacket' – addressing the issue of consumerism in the midst of the Black Friday frenzy, by inviting people to think about their consumption choices. In 2015, they launched the campaign: 'If it's broken, fix it,' while a bus toured the US and Europe, offering repairs of broken Patagonia garment.

Meanwhile, 40,000 pieces of broken garment are repaired at the Patagonia headquarters in Nevada every year. Since 2017, Patagonia has been running *wornwear*: an online shop in which customers can trade, sell and buy secondhand Patagonia goods.[7] The company also offers its clients the option of returning Patagonia products that have reached the end of their life span, in order to be recycled or repurposed – guaranteeing that the materials will not be incinerated or landfilled.

MATERIAL AND IDENTITY

Will we be finished, once producers implement the business models we have described above? Not yet. Even though *Product as a Service* solves a lot of the problems we have described, it really only constitutes a first step in the direction of our solution. Product design, business models and cultural change are fundamental elements of our envisioned transition to a Harvest Society – but so are operational procedures, material sciences and financing models.

No matter how well producers might start treating their products once they perceive them as material depots, we need more to ensure the enduring preservation of resources and materials: their identities will have to be integrated into our economic world, in the form of data. Anything without an identity simply gets lost far too easily. Even the strongest financial incentives cannot prevent that from happening – especially not in a world as complicated as ours is today.

As long as resources and materials can still be lost, we cannot seriously speak of the end of the linear economy – at best, we would create a very long line. *Product as a Service* is a giant step in the right direction, but we will still have to change our attitude towards materials, resources and products in a more fundamental way.

NOTES

1 Turntoo Website. http://turntoo.com/
2 Schaller, B. (2018). *The new automobility: Lyft, Uber and the Future of American Cities*. Retrieved from https://www.schallerconsult.com/-rideservices/automobility.htm
3 "Een Abonnement Op Wassen." *Bluemovement*. https://www.bluemovement.nl/
4 Rogers, E. M. (1962). *Diffusion of innovations*. New York: Free Press of Glencoe.

5 "Circular Denim: A World Without Waste." *Jeans*. https://mudjeans.eu/

6 A world without waste: Covering an icon in denim to be more sustainable. https://about.ikea.com/en/sustainability/a-world-without-waste/covering-an-icon-in-denim-to-be-more-sustainable

7 "Better Than New." *Worn Wear*, Patagonia. https://wornwear.patagonia.com/

I'd rather have a passport full of stamps than a house full of stuff.

(UNKNOWN)

CHAPTER SIX

The material passport

Waste is material without identity. All we need to do in order to keep material from becoming waste, is to provide it with a lasting identity that is separate from its current use. How could we organize and record this?

DOI: 10.4324/9781003258674-7

In 1713, an important book was published: *Sylvicultura oeconomica.*
Its author, Hans Carl von Carlowitz, established the concept of
Nachhaltigkeit – which, in English, has become known as *sustainability.*
In his extensive body of work, he used the term just once, but it remains
linked to his intellectual heritage forever.[1]

Von Carlowitz (1645–1714) grew up as the son of a Saxon nobleman
who was charged with the management of the mountainous forest of
the Erzgebirge: the mountain range forming a natural border between
Saxony and Bohemia. The region's lumber was indispensable to its
mining industry; among other things, it was used as fuel for the smelting
furnaces. However, at the time, the forests were being decimated on
a much bigger scale. Wood was needed for the purpose of rebuilding
houses and cities that had been destroyed by the Thirty Years' War, which
had left a devastating trail all over Europe.

Von Carlowitz foresaw that if the consumption of wood were to continue
at the same rate, the mining industry would soon be in trouble – and the
livelihoods of many of its citizens with it. Therefore, a sense of frugality
was needed with regard to the forest, or so he wrote in his book. He
emphasized the fact that wood was a daily necessity to the people in the
region, not unlike bread or water, and that it was therefore imperative to
treat the forest with care. That way, its growth rate could keep up with the
logging – allowing the people to make use of the wood constantly and
continuously. "Whenever we cut a tree, we must replace it with a new
one," he wrote. He decided that the amount of wood extracted from the
forest should never again surpass the amount of wood that was being
added through the practice of sowing and planting. His method later
became known as reforestation.

Von Carlowitz's line of thinking was a remarkably modern one.
Comparable systematic methods existed in the areas of agriculture and
horticulture, but until then such reasoning had been absent in the area
of forest management. For farmers, planting trees had never made sense:
trees grow far too slowly for farmers to enjoy the fruits of their labor
within their own lifetimes.

Mit GOtt!

SYLVICVLTVRA OECONOMICA,

Oder

Haußwirthliche Nachricht und Naturmäßige

Anweisung

Zur

Wilden Baum-Zucht,

Nebst

Gründlicher Darstellung/

Wie zu förderst durch Göttliches Benedeyen dem allenthalben und insgemein einreissenden

Grossen Holtz-Mangel/

vermittelst Säe- Pflantz- und Versetzung vielerhand Bäume zu prospiciren/ auch also durch Anflug und Wiederwachs des so wohl guten und schleunig anwachsend- als andern gewüchsig-nützlichen Holtzes, gantz öde und abgetriebene Holtz-Ländereyen, Plätze und Orte widerum Holtzreich, nütz und brauchbar zu machen; Bevorab von Saam- Bäumen und wie der wilde Baum-Saamen zu sammlen, der Grund und Boden zum Säen zuzurichten, solche Saat zu bewerckstelligen, auch der junge Anflug und Wiederwachs zubeobachten. Daneben das sogenannte lebendige, als Schlag- an Ober- und Unter-Holtz auffzubringen und zu vermehren, welchen beygefügt die Arten des Tangel- und Laub-Holtzes, theils deren Eigenschafften und was besagtes Holtz für Saamen trage, auch wie man mit frembden Baum-Gewächsen sich zu verhalten, ferner wie das Holtz zu fällen, zu verkohlen, zu äschern und sonst zu nutzen.

Alles zu nothdürfftiger Versorgung des Hauß- Bau- Brau- Berg- und Schmeltz-Wesens/ und wie eine immerwährende Holtz-Nutzung, Land und Leuten/ auch jedem Hauß-Wirthe zuunschätzbaren grossen Auffnehmen/ pfleglich und füglich zu erziehlen und einzuführen.

Vorbey zugleich eine gründliche Nachricht von den in Churfl. Sächß. Landen

Gefundenen Turff

dessen Natürliche Beschaffenheit/ grossen Nutzen/ Gebrauch und nützlichen Verkohlung.

Aus Liebe zu Beförderung des algemeinen Bestens beschrieben

Von

Hannß Carl von Carlowitz/

Königl. Pohl. und Churfl. Sächß. Cammer-Rath/ und Ober-Berg-Hauptmann.

Mit Königl. Pohl. undChufürstl. Sächß. allergnädigsten PRIVILEGIO.

LEIPZIG/
verlegts Johann Friedrich Braun 1713.

The long-term character of the rewards of reforestation therefore made it necessary to strictly regulate forest management, according to von Carlowitz. This argument did not fall on deaf ears: governments all over the world have since founded forestry commissions, whose employees are charged with preserving the forests.

USE, NOT CONSUME

As we've discussed in Chapter 3, our Earth is a closed system. Like a forest, it contains a limited amount of resources – but unlike those of a forest, most of the Earth's resources will never grow back. Once they are gone, they are gone forever. In such a system, unlimited growth is not just unlikely; it's a logical impossibility.

The long-term perspective introduced by von Carlowitz is therefore not just useful with regard to trees. Our entire economy should be transformed into a system aimed at the preservation of everything that is finite (resources, materials and land), modeled after the way von Carlowitz reformed forest management.

In order to realize this, we will have to find a way to detach economic growth and prosperity from resource *consumption* (which is not at all the same as resource *use*).

In our current economic model, tons of limited resources are lost to us forever, day after day. Information about the individual characteristics of these materials gives way to a uniform uselessness, creating what we call 'waste' – material without an identity. The *Product as a Service* business model has the power to decrease the scope of this problem, but it cannot put a stop to it; the risk of resources and materials ending up in anonymity remains substantial in today's complex economic world. If we really wish to end the planet-wide obliteration of the resources of our closed system, we will have to manage them more intelligently.

Thankfully, awareness of the staggeringly wasteful nature of the linear economy seems to be growing. Methods for retrieving resources from waste are getting more and more attention. One of such methods is called urban mining. Adherents of this practice regard cities and other densely populated areas as 'mines' – containing huge reserves of resources that can be (partially) recovered: raw materials from durable goods such as electrical appliances, cars, railways and buildings. The value hidden in these urban mines is considerable: journalists at the British independent news organization The Conversation combined the data of several open-source databases in Australia and concluded that the city of Melbourne has a stock of 1.5 million tons of accumulated resources in every square kilometer of its built environment alone (so excluding products and appliances).

However, urban mining and similar practices can only reclaim whatever can still be saved after the ecological disaster that is the linear economy – like lifeboats looking for potential survivors in the ocean surrounding a shipwreck. Nobody has kept track of *how much*, *where* and *what* can be found, since this situation was never anticipated. No lifeboats installed, no passenger list documented. In that sense, mining is an accurate metaphor indeed: mines open after the presence of a mineral resource has been established, but before there is any knowledge available regarding how much of the mineral will be found in this place, or what the risks surrounding the extraction of this mineral will be. This makes mining rather inefficient – and while we have no choice in this regard when it comes to the mining of mineral resources, we do with regard to the mining of urban resources.

In addition to the inefficiency produced by this lack of knowledge, today's products and buildings are not designed in ways that make it easy or even possible to take them apart without damaging the materials you are trying to reclaim – let alone reuse the object's individual components. The majority of products and buildings have been assembled in such intricate ways that extracting resources from them is often technically impossible or such a costly business, so that it is currently not economically feasible to do so. The ways in which they are discarded make it even more difficult to recuperate materials for the future – even if raw material prices would rise to a level where recovery would be cost-effective. While methods like urban mining can rectify some of the negative effects at the end of the line, they do nothing to alter the chain itself. They can slow the problem down, but they cannot eradicate it.

THE RESOURCE CREMATORY

Today, for the first time in human history, gold is being wasted. Previously, nearly all extracted gold was processed into jewelry or other decorative articles which, because of their considerable value, were always passed on with care – or at most remelted.

"All the gold that has been mined throughout history is still in existence in the above-ground stock," says gold expert James Turk. "That means that if you have a gold watch, some of the gold in that watch could have been mined by the Romans 2,000 years ago."

Founded in 1835, the British Geological Society advises the UK government, the public and the worlds of science and industry on all geoscientific issues. According to the BGS, about 12% of the gold mined each year is currently processed into electronic devices, the average smartphone contains about 30 mg of gold.[2] The amount used in each individual device, however, is so minimal that it is not economically viable to go through the process of extracting it from a discarded device. The majority of smartphones are simply discarded after use, or they end up spending years in kitchen drawers (only to still turn into trash afterward). According to the United States Environmental Protection Agency, Americans alone throw out $60 million worth of gold and silver each year in smartphones.[3] One ton of circuit boards is estimated to contain 40–800 times as much gold as one metric ton of ore.[4] Most of this gold is taken out of circulation, and its volume surpasses that of the amount of gold that is mined annually. Our gold supply has thus started diminishing, rather than growing.

This doesn't necessarily mean that the amount of gold on Earth is dwindling, of course: we just lose access to it. When we talk about losing things in this way, we are talking about 'losing' in a relational sense: these things are lost *to us*. They, of course, do not vanish into thin air. "What exists is uncreated and imperishable, for it is whole and unchanging and complete. It was not, nor shall it be different, since it is now, all at once, one and continuous," as the Greek philosopher Parmenides said.[5]

We lose *resources*, because the matter of which they consist is lost to us *qua resource*. It becomes inaccessible to us, because it gets too mixed up with other kinds of matter, or because it changes form (from solid to liquid or gas, for instance). Humanity would not have caused climate change if this weren't the case. That which used to be located under our feet is now hanging above our heads – in the form of CO_2.

Of course, *urban mining* is not the only solution our society has come up with. The most common and well-known is called *recycling*: the process of providing anonymous material with a new identity. The problem with recycling, however, is that, like urban mining, it is usually too expensive and thus not profitable to extract all used resources from discarded products – which means that resources are almost never used in their original form. Instead, recycling companies opt to treat vast amounts of material by incineration: a way of processing waste that involves the controlled combustion of organic substances contained in waste materials. This converts the waste into ash, flue gas and heat. The heat generated through this process can be used to generate electric power.

Though waste incineration installations start to be subject of debate, European law calls the waste incineration process 'a useful deployment of waste' – and EU member states are free to subsidize the practice. The energy generated by incinerators is often referred to as green energy, and the process of generation as 'thermal recycling.' A waste incineration plant may even be called a 'recycling plant' according to EU directives. These green-washing euphemisms describe a process that amounts to the cremation of resources that we will never get back – while we have access to an infinitely powerful source of energy hanging in the sky above our heads.

Between 2010 and 2011, the amount of waste managed by local authorities and sent to incinerators tripled in the UK. A report by the

British Green Party found that, if those trends continue, the millions of tons of waste incinerated will have overtaken the amount that is recycled by this year. In a 2018 *Guardian* interview, Green party politician Jenny Jones said:

> There is a logic to generating energy from the waste that we cannot recycle or reuse, but it is meant to be a last resort option. What we have created instead is a market-driven system of incinerators which constantly need to be fed.

Recycling companies therefore often operate *at the expense* of resources instead of *in favor* of them, as the term seems to suggest. Why does this largely go unnoticed? Because it all happens in anonymity, in an environment in which materials have neither identity, nor value or rights. That is, therefore, the first area that must change, if we really want to adapt our actions to our interests in the long term.

THE WOODEN BEAMS OF NEW COLLEGE

A beautiful example of long-term planning can be found in a famous story about the oakwood beams of New College in Oxford. Whether the story is based on facts is a point of debate, yet the story so beautifully illustrates the line of thinking we need, that it is worth to be retold. New College, one of the oldest buildings on the Oxford campus, was founded in 1379. About a century ago, it was discovered that the wooden ceiling of the dining room had been severely damaged by beetles. The beams, stretching over the entire distance of the large room, would have to be replaced as soon as possible – but where does one find oakwood beams of that size, on such short notice? Someone asked the local forest commissioner, and to everyone's great surprise, the commissioner said he had been expecting this question.

Apparently, when New College was built, some incredibly thoughtful person had suggested planting oaks that could be used to replace the wooden beams stretching over the dining room, should the wood ever start

rotting. This information had been passed on by foresters for centuries. They all knew: hands off those oak trees – they're meant for New College.[6]

Whether true or not, what we love about this story is the incredible amount of foresight demonstrated by the person who came up with a solution to a problem that wouldn't arise for several hundred years. The main reason for its success, however, lies in the fact that the information necessary to sustain it had been written down and passed on with care. There is an important lesson to learn here: want to keep something available? Document it, and it will become the material of the future.

WRITE *DOWN*, NOT *OFF*

Through the process of writing things down, we can gradually build knowledge onto knowledge. Societies that have never learned to write are significantly less developed than those that have. After all, the amount of knowledge that can be stored in writing is unlimited – whereas the amount of knowledge that can be stored in the mind of an illiterate person has been estimated to be the equivalent of about 1.5 *Iliads*.[7]

Recording collective knowledge allows generations to build onto the knowledge acquired by all the generations before it, layering knowledge upon knowledge and allowing the collective body of knowledge to reach the mindblowing level that characterizes our current scientific world. "If I have seen further than others, it was because I was standing on the shoulders of giants," Isaac Newton famously proclaimed.[8]

We tend to attribute inventions and scientific breakthroughs to individuals, while in reality every single one of them has been a collective effort that never could have happened without this ability to document valuable information. It is no coincidence that important breakthroughs often happen independently, in different places, at the same time. If we couldn't *write things down*, we would never have reached the levels of development at which we currently find ourselves. That which we discover and write down today is tomorrow's starting point.

Documenting things we consider to be valuable is something we often do intuitively. Parents consider their children to be the most valuable thing they have, regardless of the fact that they invest an average of $200,000 in them without expecting any financial return. This sentiment commonly manifests itself in a desire to document every part of their lives. We film our children's first steps, their height is documented by a little line on the kitchen wall and entire photo albums are filled with days gone by – so as to not to lose any of these precious moments.

On the other hand, that which we deem worthless, we tend to literally *write off*. In the linear economy, this is done on a massive scale. Large hotel chains, for instance, replace all of their furniture every five to seven years. The 'old' furniture is written off by that time. For most companies and organizations, the financial depreciation period is the guiding principle for investments. As soon as it ends, the machinery or furniture in question is replaced – regardless of whether it still functions or not. These financially motivated decisions account for a lot of unnecessary material loss in our economies.

Buildings that lose their current function are demolished without hesitation, which is usually quite expensive in itself, and which results in a lot of waste: both in the EU and in the US, construction and demolition waste accounts for around 40% of waste produced annually.[9] The value of the building's materials is forgotten because it was never written *down*, only written *off* until it hit zero. As soon as the accounting value of something hits zero, we automatically regard it as worthless: another one of the one-dimensional perspectives created by our financial and fiscal rules. But as we have discussed before, within a closed system, *everything* is valuable. There is no such thing as worthlessness.

ANONYMITY/IDENTITY

Anything we discover and mine has existed since long before we found it. The reason its existence seems to 'start' when it is found is because that is the point at which it receives an identity – and identity begets value. When materials are written off and end up as waste, the opposite thing happens: with their identity, their value disappears and the material is lost to us. In anonymity, everything has the same value – none.

It doesn't matter whether you're a lawyer, a Nobel prizewinner, or a teacher. If, due to circumstances, you suddenly find yourself without a passport, you enter the same boat as everyone else without one: *anonymity*. In our current world, documenting and preserving identity is immensely important. When, in times of war, governments' temporarily cannot warrant their people's identities, the population of an entire region can end up in anonymity. Those are the places in which the most dreadful crimes of war are committed. Anonymity equals the absence of rights: whether in the case of humans, areas, animals or resources.

As long as materials can still end up in anonymity, valuable resources can get lost – and as long as valuable resources get lost, our economy at large remains linear, no matter how extended. After applying all the methods described so far, we will have stretched the linear economy out as far as possible – but in the long run, we still will not have fundamentally changed its form. In order to make sure that nothing can get lost, we simply cannot afford to attempt to retrieve resources at the end of the line, using techniques like the ones described above.

Any real solution must therefore start playing a role much earlier on in the production process and must in addition be much more radical: it must prevent resources from ever ending up in anonymity in the first place. The only way to ensure that is by giving resources a permanent identity. We will have to start documenting them.

THE MATERIAL PASSPORT

In a world like ours, with such complex economic and social structures, with all the goodwill there is, we still could never be sure that nothing gets lost – unless we write everything down. We can only prevent materials from becoming anonymous waste by giving them a sustainable, recorded, documented and archived identity. Only by 'capturing' our physical world in data, we can organize finite resources in such a way that they remain accessible to us permanently.

In order to prevent more materials to be wasted, we invented the 'material passport' for buildings in 2011: a document containing a detailed inventory of all the materials, resources and components of a product or building, as well as detailed information about their location – providing materials with identities that are independent of their current use.

In 2013, the town hall of the Dutch town of Brummen became the first building in the world with a material passport. Two years earlier, our architectural office had been commissioned to renovate this historic town hall and build an extension onto it – but there was something unusual about this commission. Given the impending merger of many local communities, the local council asked us to design a temporary extension, since there is a distinct possibility that the council will not be needing a town hall anymore, a few decades from now. This was a rare case in which a temporary need was not just identified as such, but even strictly quantified: twenty years. We could not have asked for a better opportunity to implement our vision of a circular building.

All suppliers were asked to design components in such a way that they will be able to take them back after 20 years and resell them. One day, we received a phone call from the manufacturer of wooden beams that we were working with. "Would it be all right if the beams were to be three centimeters thicker than discussed?" was his question. "Of course," we replied. "But what for?" He explained that this increased thickness would increase the load-bearing capacity of the beams, which would make them useful for a much broader range of operational capabilities 20 years from now. He would be able to ask 20% more money for them than he would have been able to without these three additional centimeters. Suddenly, this supplier was forced to take a long-term perspective on his business and the materials he was selling. And while this manufacturer's wooden beam-foresight may have been projected a mere 20 years into the future – instead of several centuries – the principle is the same.

The town hall building was awarded the 2013 Architecture Award for Sustainable Architecture, a Dutch prize awarded to buildings that have achieved exceptional environmental sustainability. The new building can be entirely dismantled when the moment comes at which the town hall will lose its function. All the necessary information about its separate components and materials was documented in a material passport, providing each of the materials used with a permanent identity.

Giving something an officially recognized, documented identity allows it to receive and retain value. In some cases, this value increase is enormous – like in the case of a previously unknown painting that suddenly gets identified as a genuine Leonardo da Vinci. All identities express the uniqueness of their subjects in one way or another, however, turning them into something that transcends the sum of their characteristics.

Many years ago, Thomas's father told us an interesting story about the importance of documenting identity. In World War II many bells from church bell towers were confiscated to be melted down to supply metal for the war effort. Thomas's grandfather and father secretly made plaster casts of the inscriptions on the bells which had been taken down and stored at the railway station. The casts were kept in the grandfather's cellar for many years. In winter 1947, when a large number of bells were discovered at Hamburg's docks, those from the Oberberg district were identified conclusively from the casts and returned to the places where some of them had been hanging for centuries.

An identity turns an object, person or resource into something that should not be lost, something in need of protection. Our sense of responsibility for what happens with someone or something strongly correlates with whether that person or thing possesses such an identity. Much of our collective denial of environmental issues can be explained by the fact that the things we lose through our reckless economic behavior are mostly anonymous: the lives of nameless future humans, ecosystems and raw materials. Once something acquires a name, it becomes much harder to ignore.

This is exactly where the material passport comes in: it puts an end to anonymity. With it, we will be able to eliminate all waste. Or course, we will still have organic waste – banana peels, coffee grounds – but that consists mostly of resources that are in fact unlimited, so long as we treat them in the spirit of Hans Carl von Carlowitz. We will thereby acknowledge that everything is equally important: human, animal, plant and material.

BUILDINGS AS MATERIAL MINES

Providing every new building with a material passport allows us to make a lot of progress: approximately 40% of the buildings expected to exist in 2050, have yet to be built. However, if we can take stock of the resources and materials used for the construction of all *existing* buildings, the effect would be even bigger. If we can develop a sense of respect for supposedly worthless, depreciated buildings, these buildings will turn into an interesting source of value.

To safeguard materials for the future, we need to record which ones have been used in a building, what quantities and where. With this in mind, we have taken advantage of a tool widely used by architects, engineers and construction firms, Building Information Modelling (3D BIM). This is a smart process based on a 3D model that provides information and tools for the efficient planning, design, construction and management of buildings and infrastructure.

We used 3D BIM to develop the material passport mentioned above as a data model. It collects, documents and stores all the information on the materials used in construction. In this way, we always know what materials were incorporated in a product or component: how many kilograms of steel, gold, copper or ceramic material, for instance. It also records where the materials came from, whether they were processed and if so how, and where in the building they are at present. Every detail of the building, however large or small, is noted, thus preventing it from ending up as waste once it leaves its original location.

At the present time, someone who needs to get rid of an existing building goes about this by calling a demolition firm and receiving a substantial bill in return. If that person is in possession of a material passport, however, their depreciated building suddenly gains value again, meaning they might not have to pay for the demolition at all – and in some cases might even make money from it! This principle applies to all buildings, everywhere in the world. We call this principle *Buildings as Material Mines*.

To give you an example of this: we were recently approached by a large company, and were asked to help them solve something they were struggling with: they needed to get rid of an enormous building on their property. In one of the following meetings, we routinely asked how much money would be gained by demolishing this building.

"Gained?" they replied, confused. "The demolition *costs* us €1.5 million!"

Since the building had been depreciated down to zero book-value, the company had automatically assumed that it had become entirely worthless. It was not, of course.

To prove them wrong, we spent the next two weeks 'mapping' the building as a mine: we identified all the materials used, took stock of them, and estimated their value. We ended up identifying about €600,000 in materials value, which our client still could capitalize.

At a conference, we met a contractor from Austria who told us that whenever he constructs a building, he immediately registers the right of first refusal for its materials – anticipating the moment the building will lose its function. Gradually, people seem to be starting to realize what value is hidden in these buildings.

BUILDINGS AS MATERIAL DEPOTS

A second way of using material passports follows a principle we refer to as the *Buildings as Material Depots* principle. When a building is designed in a way that materials can be taken out again, it automatically turns into a kind of depot for materials: a storage of resources, kept safe for future use. As we explained above, every building is in essence a material depot, however unorganized – unless we knock it down the minute it stops fulfilling our temporary need. However, the difference between *mine* and *depot* is determined by the amount of thinking ahead: buildings that were built for disassembly and equipped with material passport in hand are *depots*, buildings that were built without these qualities are *mines*.

Obviously, material depots are many times more efficient than material mines – even beside the fact that we know what's in them, and where everything is located and how to retrieve it. After all, if we register the materials and resources that will go into a building *before* it has been built, we can use this information to influence the design and construction process, thus ensuring that all materials can easily and safely be taken out of the building at some point – without losing any of their value. This will give rise to a whole new market of reusable products, components, and materials that make building, renovating, and dismantling buildings as easy as possible.

Buildings as Material Depots is the guiding principle for projects we realize with our studio RAU Architects. In 2012 RAU Architects was asked to design the energy company Alliander's new head office, a large-scale redevelopment of an existing office complex from the 1960, which should be capable of serving as a modern office space for 1,500 employees. Instead of tearing the existing buildings down as the client had envisioned, we convinced him of creating the world's first energy positive and circular office building. Together with the team we formulated the ambition that we would preserve 90% of the existing material on site, use as much secondary material as possible and ensure that all virgin material could be reused after the building's end of life. Every resource and material used for its construction was registered in a material passport, and its design allows for every component to be 'harvested' at all times – without losing any of its value.

The greatest challenge was to find a company that could provide us with the large steel roof construction that was designed to cover and unite the

existing buildings into one single structure. Traditional steel construction companies did not understand our requirements for a roof construction enabling easy assembly, disassembly, transport and reassembly, while guaranteeing safety at the same time. Ultimately, we found the solution outside of the construction sector, after asking ourselves what kind of company we could think of that faces a similar challenge. We suddenly had it: a company building roller coasters.

The result looks like a horizontal roller coaster – and not only did it meet all the circular requirements we were looking for, it also used 30% less steel than traditional constructions would have needed.[10]

Another interesting fact about circular building that we discovered was the fact that, due to prefabrication and modularization, not only construction time and risk/cost could be reduced but also the impact on the building site as such. A beautiful example is a bird observatory we designed for a very sensitive Nature area on the coast of the Dutch Haringvliet. The egg-shaped building, consisting of 402 wooden beams, was prefabricated in Finland, using a file-to-factory system, and then shipped to its location – where it was assembled on-site and covered with locally sourced reed. Designed as a temporary structure, it will be easy to take into its parts again and move to a different location if required.[11]

These buildings meet all our core objectives: we anticipated temporality (nobody knows how long the need for these buildings will remain) and we made sure that no materials or resources could be lost, through the use of a material passport. The buildings are thus in complete harmony with the principles of our closed system.

BUILDINGS AS MATERIAL BANKS

As soon as we see that buildings are in essence material depots, we can take things even further: we can stop depreciating buildings to zero, as is dictated by the logic of our current economic model. The material value of buildings will be *written down*, rather than *written off*.

If we not only register the *location* of specific materials but also estimate and register their *value*, we can turn a building into a kind of 'material bank.' The conserved material value of a building (the sum of the value of all resources temporarily stored inside it) can amount to up to 15% to 20% of the total cost invested in constructing the building. Its real economic value may end up being much higher than that, of course – time will tell. The rest (labor, energy) is lost, but those are unlimited resources, meaning we will always be able to replace them. Our *limited* resources, on the other hand, should be treated with utmost care.

An important condition with regard to conserving value is, again, that buildings must be designed and constructed in ways that make it easy, and therefore economically worthwhile, to dismantle them and reuse the materials and resources stored in them. This will translate into a financial incentive for developers, producers and builders to anticipate temporality right from the start.

This most advanced application of a building as a materials bank has been put into practice for the first time for another client – very appropriately – the Dutch Triodos Bank. The bank's new headquarters were built entirely according to the principles of the model we have discussed so far.[12]

Triodos Bank was founded in the Netherlands in 1980 with the aim of creating a sustainable banking culture. It arose from an initiative on the part of members of the Dutch economic and financial community with a social conscience, who came together to find out how money can be managed sustainably. Since then, Triodos Bank has done pioneering work in many areas, for example, the funding of renewable energy, microfinance and a green finance fund. *The Financial Times* described Triodos as the most sustainable bank in the world a few years ago, so it comes as no surprise that the bank's building should reflect the same spirit. Back in 1996, RAU Architects built the bank's first headquarters, when Triodos commissioned a building of its own for the first time in its history. It goes without saying that this was the most sustainable building in the Netherlands at the time, energy-optimized and with a façade built of reused brick. In 2019, Triodos inaugurated its third building designed by RAU Architects, this time conceived as a material bank. The timber structure is held together by 165,312 screws and can be dismantled completely and rebuilt elsewhere. All the materials used were selected based on strict recyclability criteria and recorded in a material passport, and their value is constantly monitored. It is not so much an immovable as a movable property, a material bank with a future: a bank within a bank, as it were.

Material passports alone cannot guarantee that no materials can get lost, however. Documents possess little value if they are not acknowledged by an official institution. That applies to material passports as well as personal passports. Any document of identification derives its value from being registered and recognized by an official body. Without this backing, documents are just pieces of paper – not unlike money.

NOTES

1 Carlowitz, H. C. (1713). *Sylvicultura oeconomica: Anweisisungen zur wilden Baumzucht.* Johann Friedrich Braun, Leipzig.
2 Prior, E. (2016). How much gold is there in the world? *BBC News.* https://www.bbc.com/news/magazine-21969100
3 Jaiswal, A., Samuel, C., Patel, B. S., & Kumar, M. (2015). "Go Green with WEEE: Eco-friendly approach for handling E-waste." *Procedia Computer Science*, Vol. 46, 1317–1324.
4 Voakes, G. (2012). *The lesser-known facts about e-waste recycling.* Hack College, Business Insider. https://www.businessinsider.com/the-lesser-known-facts-about-e-waste-recycling-2012-10?international=true&r=US&IR=T Bankmycell (2019). *Cell phone recycling & e-waste facts.* rhttps://www.bankmycell.com/support/e-waste-cell-phone-recycling-facts#stats2
5 Palmer, J. (2016). "Parmenides." *Stanford Encyclopedia of Philosophy*. Stanford University. Retrieved from https://plato.stanford.edu/entries/parmenides/
6 Brand, S. (2012). How buildings learn: The oak beams of New College Oxford. Retrieved from https://www.youtube.com/watch?v=YqH4eWR7jDQ
7 Bard, A., & Söderqvist, J. (2012). *The futurica trilogy.* Stockholm: Stockholm Texts.

8 Deming, D. (2010). *Science and technology in world history, Volume 1: "The ancient world and classical civilization."* Jefferson, NC: McFarland & Company.

9 UNEP. Energy efficiency for buildings. Paris. http://www.studiocollantin.eu/pdf/UNEP%20Info%20sheet%20-%20EE%20Buildings.pdf

10 Aguilar, C. (2015). Alliander HQ/RAU architects. *ArchDaily*, ArchDaily. Retrieved from www.archdaily.com/777783/alliander-hq-rau-architects

11 Astbury, J. (2019). Thatched reeds cover egg-shaped Tij observatory for watching birds. *Dezeen*, Dezeen, 17 June 2019. https://www.dezeen.com/2019/05/11/tij-bird-observatory-rau-architects-scheelhoek-nature-reserve/

12 Tapia, D. (2019). Triodos Bank/RAU architects. *ArchDaily*, ArchDaily. https://www.archdaily.com/926357/triodos-bank-rau-architects

A library outranks any other one thing a community can do to benefit its people. It is a never failing spring in the desert.

(ANDREW CARNEGIE)

CHAPTER SEVEN

Madaster – a registry for materials

Material passports are a way to document the identity of materials, but without a central registry they would be like library books without a librarian.

DOI: 10.4324/9781003258674-8

Let us look at another registered, documented and well-archived *limited edition* in our closed system: the surface of our planet. We carefully measure, describe and keep track of who owns which part of it, whether they be countries, companies or individuals. On Google Maps, we can look up exactly how big any given country is and where its internationally agreed-upon borders are located. Of course, these borders change from time to time (voluntarily as well as involuntarily), but the total surface of the planet will always be about 510 million km^2, of which 30% land and 70% water. In addition, most countries document the ownership of every piece of land within their national borders. This is continuously registered, documented and archived in a so-called *cadastre or registry of deeds*: a public institution for the registration of land ownership.

A system like this is important to a peaceful society. It prevents your neighbor from building a shed in your garden, and a neighboring company from deciding that your family home will have to be demolished to make space for an extension of their industrial site. In this, registry can be found how big any given piece of land is, to whom it belongs and since when it has belonged to that person or organization.

It thus functions as a standardized but dynamic data library with which governments keep track of who owns what, when. In densely populated (developed) countries, normally not a single square meter is unaccounted for. Greece is the only EU member-state without a complete national land registry. Since 1994, millions of EU-funds went into creating this land-registry, in 2018, only 8% of the land was registered, and although land registration had to be completed in 2021 and an electronic Greek cadastre has been established even municipalities are struggling to register their property. When neither the state nor private landowners or businesses know exactly which piece of land belongs to whom, the result is legal chaos, uncertain investors, tax evasion and illegal construction sites. A situation which for long was detrimental to the Greek economy.[1]

Registration in the cadastre is not just a helpful tool for landowners: it is obligatory by law, and for good reason. The confusion that arose after the fall of Communism in many countries is a good example of what happens when land ownership is not well-documented. In countries like Romania, this remains a problem to this day. For over a decade now, Transylvania's forest – including Europe's last virgin forests – have been illegally logged, against the will of local communities. This has been facilitated almost entirely by the confusing situation that arose when formerly expropriated lands were suddenly privatized again. The lack of registration and organization made it possible for anyone to claim huge swaths of land, using forged property deeds in order to then sell 'their' land to the highest bidder. As we mentioned earlier, anonymity begets unlawful actions – whether related to the treatment of people, material or land.[2]

MADASTER

In order to make sure that materials will be able to continue playing their part in our economic world, independent of the products/buildings they temporarily constitute, their identities must be clear, tradeable and provable. That means that we can't just give them identification documents: those documents need to be registered in a central archive, too. For that purpose, we will need a new public institution.

Think of the way a library works: through the process of documenting who borrows which book when, books remain accessible generation after generation. Every book has an identity – a symbol – which, in its physical absence, represents it within the confines of a well-ordered system. This permanent identity allows for the library to keep track of the whereabouts of their books, so that it isn't necessary for the library to keep the books on the shelf at all times. Instead, its book collection is always spread out over the shelves, backpacks, cars, workplaces and nightstands of its various members.

Another public institution that tracks changing possessions or ownership of limited editions is the land registry or cadaster.

How would an economy in which materials have independent identities registered in an official registry work, exactly? That is easiest to explain if we take the construction industry as an example – not an insignificant sector in terms of resource consumption. In addition to accounting for approximately 40% of all waste produced in the US and the EU, it also uses around 40% of all resources worldwide.[3] In the UK and the EU, in spite of a recycling rates of over 90%, this enormous material stream is currently mainly downcycled[4] most demolition material from buildings is used as aggregate in road-building, not for new buildings. In the city of Amsterdam alone, according to a study, material to the value of €688 million is released from renovation and demolition work, and 50% of that value is lost through downcycling[5] – despite the fact that the Netherlands is a leader in the reuse of secondary raw materials.[6]

Even if the construction sector were the only sector we could convince to use a registered material passport, the effects would be unprecedented. To utilize this gigantic potential, we need to regard the built environment as a store of materials and consciously steer their use, organize material streams and close material cycles. This means to perceive existing structures as material mines and designing new ones as material depots, furnishing them with a permanent identity, a material passport, which is registered in a public registry like a library or cadastre in order to facilitate reuse at the end of a building's life.

For that reason – and because of our background – the construction sector is where we have begun putting our theory into practice first. We believe in practical action, so rather than just writing and talking about this idea – in the hope that our government might take action to bring about this much-needed public institution – we decided to found the cadastre for materials – Madaster – ourselves. It is set up as an online public database in which the identity and temporary location of materials are documented in the form of material passports, making sure their identities are recognized and acknowledged at all times.

Following the foundation of Madaster on February 17, 2017, by an interdisciplinary expert team, with functional and expert support from organizations in the construction industry, after a seven-month development period the platform went online on 29 September 2017, providing access for private individuals, firms, authorities and academics. By summer 2022, the platform is in operation in the Netherlands, Switzerland, Germany, Norway, Denmark, Finland, Belgium and Austria. An additional four national Madaster entities are currently under development and projects are being registered across the globe.

Madaster provides a platform as a service (PaaS) subscription that produces a 'materials passport' for every registered building, which itemizes the materials and quantities used, the quality of materials and locations and their monetary value. It also calculates a 'circularity index' against which each material passport is scored, so one can see what percentage of materials can be reused.

The platform's software is able to generate material passports for buildings automatically. It works by extracting and analyzing data from the BIM as well as other import formats that an organization uploads when it registers a new building. Madaster connects to a large number of external databases to enable the BIM information to be matched and enriched with additional data sources, such as product databases and financial data from the London Metal exchange, for example.

The platform assesses materials, material composition, structural connections, etc. based on predefined criteria, producing a 'digital twin' of the building that provides important information on its maintenance and renovation and the reusability of the materials. The data can also be used for ESG (sustainability) reporting by property holders, who can use data generated by Madaster – e.g., the building's CO_2 footprint – as an aid to simplifying processes and solving problems faster. Jürg Schneider, former head of Sustainability Real Estate for SBB (Swiss Railways), and one of the first Madaster partners in Switzerland, says he regards Madaster as an important tool for sustainable building management.

A circularity index indicates the extent to which reusability is guaranteed by the design and processing of materials. This is, in turn, reflected in the financial valuation that the platform's software carries out. The platform

DE KUBUS

ALGEMEEN   ▶ GEBOUW   BOUWPROCES   CIRCULARITEIT   DOSSIER

FILTER

TOTALEN

LOCATIE

CONSTRUCTIE

OMHULLING

TECHNISCHE
INSTALLATIES

AFBOUW

TOTALEN   91,87 m3   0 m3   24,01 m3   5,26 m3   0,04 m3   0,17 m3
163,96 t   0 t   57,76 t   5,49 t   0 t   0,31 t

76%
69,56 m3
153,95 t

0%
0 m3
0 t

100%
23,99 m3
57,58 t

64%
3,38 m3
5,46 t

0%
0 m3
0 t

100%
0,17 m3
0,31 t

0
0
0

12%
11,15 m3
0,19 t

0%
0 m3
0 t

0%
0 m3
0 t

36%
1,88 m3
0,03 t

0%
0 m3
0 t

0%
0 m3
0 t

0%
0 m3
0 t

0%
0 m3
0 t

0%
0 m3
0 t

0%
0 m3
0 t

0%
0 m3
0 t

0%
0 m3
0 t

0%
0 m3
0 t

0%
0 m3
0 t

has a complex algorithm that calculates the current material value of the building based on up-to-date and historical financial and market data. We expect the circularity index to influence the design of buildings toward maximum reusability: the higher a building's circularity index, the higher the value of the materials used when the 'Building' option expires.

This is useful for building owners, investors and banks, which can thus improve their real estate's risk profile. We also expect the residual material value of a building to be included on the balance sheet in future – rather than being written off as at present – thus having a positive effect on many companies' profit and loss accounts. This may sound like a gimmick, but it isn't: "Any substantial values involved should be taken into account in scrupulous financial reporting," says Klaus-Peter Naumann, board spokesman of the Institut der Wirtschaftsprüfer (Institute of Public Auditors) in Düsseldorf. 'Settling for less is not an option.' Already in the shipping industry, containers are not written off but written down to their scrap value, for instance. Why should this not be possible with steel girders and timber structures?[7]

Key support for the development of Madaster is currently being provided by investors buying and holding property portfolios. "The circular economy is becoming more and more important for us. Big investors are increasingly asking about their portfolios' ecological footprints," says Sarah Krüger, sustainability manager at Commerz Real. "Madaster is anticipating developments that the legislators could impose on the industry." Here Krüger is thinking, e.g., of EU regulations on sustainability, which could soon bear down more on material consumption and climate-changing emissions over buildings' entire life cycles.[8]

By enabling architects and designers to use the platform for simulation, they can see how much material there is in the building or make a simulation of a building before it's even built. By uploading 3D models, organizations can see their Circular Scores and understand how they will change over time. By adjusting the proposed materials, products, and construction methods, architects and designers can improve outcomes before they begin building. The same is true for facility management, helping them understand the ongoing maintenance costs before making a purchase or embarking on construction.

THE MADASTER FOUNDATION

Registering, documenting, and archiving the materials that constitute our complex physical-social world is not an easy task: the amount of work that goes into the creation of even a single material passport is enormous.

Thankfully, our technological sophistication has been growing in recent decades, almost in exact proportion to the complexity of our modern physical world: we are inventing ever-more efficient ways of automating processes that used to depend on the actions and computing power of humans. Effective automation does require a measure of standardization, however – a library in which all librarians work according to their own filing method will certainly become a mess. To oversee the development of standards relating to the documentation of materials, we have therefore also founded the Madaster Foundation: an independent, public non-profit organization that will supervise and moderate the Madaster platform.

It has been set up in collaboration with experts from the construction, IT, finance and process-management sectors, and received initial funding from 33 companies that supported the initiative in terms of knowledge and finance. The foundation's objective is simple: the 100% elimination of waste from our economy, by means of documenting all materials.[9]

As we've explained, every material passport in the Madaster offers an overview of information regarding the materials used for the construction of a building: their location, financial value and their individual possibilities regarding reuse.

In addition, due to the calculation of a Circularity Index, every passport will contain information about the amount of thought architects and manufacturers have given to the possible reuse of the materials – as manifested in the design and production process of this particular building or product. The Circularity Index affects the financial evaluation of the building or product, transforming it into a powerful instrument for steering design and production processes in the direction of the circular economy. The higher the Circularity Index, the higher the value of the materials in the building, and thus the higher the value of the entire building.

Privacy is critical if organizations are to trust Madaster with sensitive information about their buildings. Using proven technology to ensure the privacy and ownership of the data was a major concern for the development of the database, which is why Madaster decided to use Microsoft Azure for its platform development. While it is important to store information on materials for future reuse, during the time the building is in use, confidentiality is an important requirement. The information on the Madaster platform on an individual building is therefore owned by, and will only be accessible to the building owner himself, who can decide when and how much information he decides to share publicly, comparable to the information in a communal registry, where citizens can access only their own personal data. If a building were to be demolished or dismantled, the owner could decide to share information with a secondary material marketplace or inform the manufacturers that their products or raw materials are available once again.

Since its launch in September 2017 already over 15 million square meters of buildings have been equipped with a material passport. In this way, a sizeable repository of material data, organized by location, will gradually come into being – a public library of materials for the built environment. With Madaster – which is publicly accessible – we are creating a secure foundation for preventing materials from disappearing into anonymity. This will transform our buildings into material mines, depots and banks. In this way, we are meeting our main challenge: by using data, intelligence and energy, we make finite resources infinitely available.

So far, the platform's focus has been limited to documenting the materials in the built environment, which constitutes for approximately

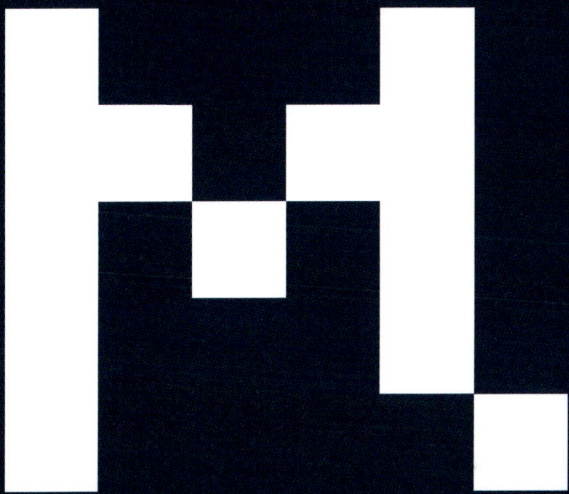

® MADASTER

40% of all material use. However, we are in the process of expanding its possibilities to include the materials of infrastructure and products. Eventually, we hope to create a library containing information about *all* the materials that move about in our economic world. In order to realize this scenario, producers will need to move from selling products to selling service contracts – and create material passports for all the goods they manufacture. That way, they will develop endless business models, all the while preserving the limited materials and resources of Spaceship Earth.

The judges of the Digital Top 50 Awards (conferred by Google, McKinsey and Rocket Internet) are also convinced of the significance of this concept for our economic system: Madaster received the Digital Top 50 Award for Social Impact in 2018. This leaves us with one question, however: can we actually safeguard the identity of materials without thinking about their rights?

NOTES

1 Cleppe, P. (2015). The case of the Greek Land Registry. *Open Europe*, Open Europe. https://openeurope.org.uk/today/blog/reforming-greece-easier-said-done-never-ending-case-land-registry/

   Lefteris, P. (2019). End in sight for Greece's long quest to complete National Land Registry. *Reuters*, Thomson Reuters. https://www.reuters.com/article/us-greece-landregistry-idUSKCN1QW23B

   Lialios, G. (2021). Municipalities Ignoring Land Registry. *EKathimerini.com*, ΚΑΘΗΜΕΡΙΝΕΣ ΕΚΔΟΣΕΙΣ ΜΟΝΟΠΡΟΣΩΠΗ Α.Ε. Εθν.Μακαρίου & Φαληρέως. https://www.ekathimerini.com/news/261830/municipalities-ignoring-land-registry/

2 EIA (2015). Stealing the last forest. Environmental Investigation Agency. https://www.illegal-logging.info/sites/files/chlogging/EIA%20(2015)%20Romania%20Report.pdf

3 UNEP. Energy efficiency for buildings. Paris. http://www.studiocollantin.eu/pdf/UNEP%20Info%20sheet%20-%20EE%20Buildings.pdf

4 Ruuska, A., & Häkkinen, T. (2014). Material efficiency of building construction. *Buildings*, Vol. 4(3), pp. 266–294. https://doi.org/10.3390/buildings4030266

5 Romers, G., & Duijvestein, P., et al. (2020). *Circulaire business cases in de MRA*. Bouw en Sloopafval. https://www.metabolic. nl/publications/circulaire-business-cases-mra-bouw-sloopafval/

6 EU Circular Material Use Rate. Eurostat, 12 March 2020. https://ec.europa. eu/eurostat/web/products-eurostat-news/-/ddn-20200312-1

7 Mattauch, C. (2021). Eine Datenbank, die das Bauen revolutionieren könnte, Süddeuttsche Zeitung. https://www.sueddeutsche. de/wirtschaft/bauen-gebaeude-material-datenbank-madaster-1.5404136

8 Mattauch, C. (2021). Eine Datenbank, die das Bauen revolutionieren könnte, Süddeuttsche Zeitung. https://www.sueddeutsche. de/wirtschaft/bauen-gebaeude-material-datenbank-madaster-1.5404136

9 Madaster. https://www.madaster.com/en
  Madaster Foundation. https://madasterfoundation.com/

The permanent member with a final veto is Nature.
(ERIK DE RUIJTER)

CHAPTER EIGHT

UDMR – the Universal Declaration of Material Rights

The fact that each human life comes with a set of Universal Rights has become self-evident. But what about the materials that make these lives possible? What would happen if we granted Universal Rights to materials – and protect them from becoming waste?

DOI: 10.4324/9781003258674-9

On October 24, 1945, in the wake of World War II (WWII), the United Nations (UN) was founded. The intergovernmental organization was established to protect future generations from the destructive consequences of international conflict – consequences that then formed a tangible reality in large parts of the world at that moment. Six different organizations were established: the General Assembly, the UN Secretariat, the International Court of Justice, the Security Council, the Trusteeship Council and the Economic and Social Council (ECOSOC).

The ECOSOC was charged with the important task of assembling commissions that would work toward the protection of human rights in economic and social issues. One of those commissions became the Commission for Human Rights of the United Nations – chaired by the former first lady Eleanor Roosevelt, who had been sent to the United Nations as a delegate after the death of her husband, Franklin D. Roosevelt. Representatives from all over the world congregated to formulate, for the first time in history, Universal Human Rights.

"We stand today at the threshold of a great event, both in the life of the United Nations and in the life of mankind," she said on December 10, 1948, during her speech at the UN General Assembly, where the document was to be officially accepted by the United Nations. The General Assembly called on all member states to publish the declaration, "to make sure that it is spread, shown, read and clarified, especially in schools and other educational institutions, without discrimination based on political status, or nations, or regions."[1]

The notion that each human being deserves judicial protection on the grounds of nothing more than their humanity is thus a relatively young idea – younger than many people's grandparents. Of course, the Universal Declaration of Human Rights does have its roots in many ancient traditions and documents, but it wasn't until about half a century ago that the Universal Rights really appeared on the international agenda and were officially documented. Before that time, people derived their identities from the fact that they were part of a group: a family, a people, a religion, a class, a community or a state; human rights were distributed by whoever

was in charge. When people lost their membership of the group, their rights were lost along with it.

The UDHR was not the first document to attempt to record general human rights, however. Among its predecessors were the *Magna Carta and The Charter of the Forest* (1215), the *English Bill of Human Rights* (1689), the French *Déclaration des Droits de l'Homme et du Citoyen* (1789) and the American *Constitution and Bill of Rights* (1791). The policies that were grounded in these documents, however, were always limited to a specific (national) area, and usually excluded large portions of the population: women, people with a different skin color, and specific religious, political and economic groups. The documentation of the *Universal* Human Rights, therefore, was a giant step in the direction of a world in which no human being can ever find themselves without the protection of rights any more. Humans cannot 'lose' their humanness.

THE RIGHT TO RIGHTS

Worldwide, millions of people have no nationality. Legally, they don't 'belong' anywhere. They can lay claim only to a limited number of rights, are vulnerable to exploitation and discrimination, and are always at risk of getting stuck in an immigrant detention center for an undetermined period of time – reason enough for the UN, EU and Council of Europe to worry. For most people, however, national identity is simply a given. The fundamental right to reside in our 'own country' and to return to it whenever we have gone abroad is derived from our nationality. The right to a nationality is often described as 'the right to rights' for that reason.

Stateless persons cannot derive their rights from their nation. They lack a document that is of fundamental importance in today's world: a passport, a documentation of their identity. The Universal Human Rights as defined by the UDHR, however, are separated from nationality. They protect each human being, whether they are in possession of a nationality or not. At the same time, Article 15 of the UDHR states that every human being has the right to a nationality and thus to a passport. Each person in the world, therefore, theoretically has a right to rights.

THE UNIVERSAL DECLARATION OF MATERIAL RIGHTS

In the way that the rights of human beings used to be linked to the official membership of a particular group, or at least to a group identity, the rights of materials today are still completely dependent on a temporary role in a bigger whole.

A material is only granted an identity for as long as it is part of a group of materials that together form a product or a building. When this role (i.e. that of intermediate product) or the group identity (i.e., 'laptop' or 'apartment building') expire, all the individual materials and resources end up in anonymity. They don't have an identity of their own and thus become, in a metaphorical sense, stateless.

This results in the large-scale destruction and loss of the valuable resources and materials in our finite supply. Material without an identity simply becomes anonymous waste. In anonymity everything is worth the same: nothing. To prevent this from happening, we advocate a Material Passport: a registered identity for materials together with a set of fundamental rights for materials.

Ever since the acknowledgment of the Universal Declaration of Human Rights, it has been commonly accepted that we all have rights that are separate from our documented identity – rights we simply derive from being human. The acknowledgment of those rights was born out of the atrocities of WWII and the all-encompassing destruction inherent in the atomic bomb, which made humanity aware of her potential for self-destruction. The current destruction of the natural world, however, has reached levels that could be compared to those of the destructions of WWII both in scope and scale. Alongside the ever-present threat of nuclear war, the biggest threat for the sustained survival of our civilization lurks in the way we treat our environment. The way we treat our materials today is comparable to the way large groups of human beings have been treated in the past: they are being violated, abused, burned and discarded. Materials form the very foundation to our lives here on Earth, but they do not enjoy any form of legal protection and can be systematically violated and destroyed with absolute impunity.

When we acknowledge how vital materials are to our existence, however, we will be forced to stop regarding them as disposable and to stop treating them as such. Once we start striving towards an economy based on a healthy relationship between humans and the Earth, the final consequence must be that we grant materials some of the rights we have granted ourselves.

All humans are equal, after all, is not that far in meaning from *everything is equally important* – Nature's adage. What sovereignty and dignity are to humans are inviolability and utility to materials and resources. Therefore, this document is a pledge for a *Universal Declaration of Material Rights: UDMR.*

The rights registered in this document are conceptually closely related to those registered in the Universal Declaration of Human Rights. The right to an identity (the 'right to rights') prevents materials from turning into waste, in the way, the human rights equivalent prevents humans from turning into stateless persons.

Comparable to the way we don't want humans to be traumatized and undergo irreversible harm, we need to protect materials from losing their utility. Under the influence of chemical processes, the structure and composition of materials can change. If valuable materials are lost to us in this process, this is an infringement of a material's right to inviolability.

This will involve a shift in perspective that is both ethical and practical. In the first place, acknowledging the UDMR will change our attitude towards materials, resources and Nature in general. It will help us rebuild an attitude of respect toward the things that facilitate our lives, and force us to take responsibility for the permanent consequences of our actions.

Translating the articles of the Universal Declaration of Human Rights to the Universal Declaration of Material rights would provide us with a framework for a new economic system based on the preservation of resources, which is currently referred to as a circular economy. Circular economy is focused on system solutions to restructure the linear economy system that is driving environmental degradation through the acceleration of natural resource use. A circular economy approach would 'decouple' natural resource use from meeting the economic needs of the global population with a focus on social issues of jobs and social equity.

Acknowledging material rights will prevent materials from legally ending up in anonymity. This will bring us closer to a world in which the resources and materials of our closed system will be kept available to us forever. Human rights and material rights are inseparable. Our resource and material consumption has serious economic, ecological and political consequences – both in the short and in the long term. They form a threat to the sustained existence of human life on Earth that is at least as big and imminent as the threat inherent in nuclear weapons.

CLIMATE CHANGE

Though not obvious at first sight, resource consumption is closely linked to climate change. Different studies have shown that preservation of materials could significantly contribute to the reduction of greenhouse gases, as resource extraction accounts for roughly three-quarters of the energy consumption of industrial output.

It is widely acknowledged that measures determined under the Paris Climate Agreement are inadequate to achieve the goal of limiting the temperature rise of the global climate at 1.5–2.0°C. Analysis has concluded that an economy approach based on the preservation of resources (a circular economy) could reduce the gap between the Paris Agreement and the goals set by it by 50%.[2] Similarly, a circular economy approach can address the nexus between water and land. For example, a study concluded that a circular economy approach could save up to

20.2 billion cubic meters of water annually in municipal, industrial and agricultural sectors in Bangladesh alone.[3]

WAR AND PEACE

Human rights and material rights also meet *directly*, daily – in the geopolitical dimension of war and peace. With increased scarcity and increased cost to access raw materials, conflicts (cross-border) are likely to be exacerbated. And the extraction of those resources, in turn, provide the means for armed conflict. The wood from Liberia, diamonds from Sierra Leone and gold and cobalt from the Congo, all play leading roles in the gruesome civil wars that have been tearing apart that region for decades. Access and control of raw material sources and critical materials (rare earth metals) has been identified in the national security plans of over 20 countries. According to the UN, "The challenges associated with preventing, managing and resolving natural resource-induced conflicts may well come to define global peace and security in the 21st century."[4]

THE CO-VIOLATION OF RIGHTS

Also in the extraction of materials from the Earth, human rights are being violated on a daily basis, ranging from unsafe working conditions for miners, child labor and the expulsion of indigenous people from their homelands, which, in turn, contributes to the number of displaced persons, and their poverty and conflict – only for these materials to end up in drawers and waste incineration plants in a matter of years, months, sometimes even days.

The way we treat resources is anything but politically neutral – and reaches far beyond ecological consequences. If we can make our economies less dependent on importing scarce resources and materials (from conflict zones), the impact on human lives will be huge. Human

rights and material rights are thus not just closely linked in a conceptual way, but also in a very real, empirical sense: the violation of human rights and the destruction of Nature often go hand in hand.

That constitutes another reason to democratize and 'ecologize' our economies – bringing them back into harmony with the laws and regularities of Nature. If we can find a way of keeping materials in the loop, rather than using them as disposable fuel and steadily diminishing our total supply, we will improve the lives of countless people living on Earth today and guarantee a livable environment for future generations all over the world. When industrialized countries become less dependent on the supply of scarce resources from our world's conflict zones, the impact on those conflicts will be significant.

MATERIAL RIGHTS AND SUSTAINABLE DEVELOPMENT GOALS

Codifying rights for materials could significantly contribute to advancing progress in the Sustainable Development Goals (SDGs) through a circular economy approach. Achieving SDG 12 – Sustainable Production and Consumption – is only possible through replacing the current 'take, make, waste' linear economic model with a circular economy model. Moreover, such a system-wide approach, if done in an integrated fashion and with rigorous measurement, can also advance other SDGs such as SDG 2 – Zero Hunger; SDG 6 – Clean Water and Sanitation; SDG 7 – Clean Energy; SDG 8 – Good Jobs and Economic Growth; SDG 11 – Sustainable Cities and Communities; and SDG 14 – Life Below Water.[5]

It has become impossible to imagine our world without human rights: they are important topics on the agenda of every political or diplomatic consideration, and they have fundamentally changed the way people are treated in many parts of the world. Via the UDMR, we want to achieve the same thing with regard to our materials and resources. That's why in December 2018, at the 70th birthday of the UDHR, we presented the UDMR to the United Nations, accompanied by the following message:

The Earth is the only lawful owner of all resources and materials – because there is just one true permanent member in possession of a veto: Nature.

The full text of the UDMR can be found in Appendix 1 on page 215.

NOTES

1 Eleanor Roosevelt: Address to the United Nations General Assembly (1948). http://www.kentlaw.edu/faculty/bbrown/classes/HumanRightsSP10/CourseDocs/2EleanorRoosevelt.pdf

2 Sitra (2018). *The circular economy – A powerful force for climate mitigation, Transformative innovation for prosperous and low-carbon industry*. Stockholm: Material Economics Sverige AB. https://www.sitra.fi/en/publications/circular-economy-powerful-force-climate-mitigation/

3 Hieminga, G. (2017). *Circular solutions to water shortage*. ING Economics Department. https://www.ing.nl/media/ING_EBZ_circular-solutions-to-water-shortage_tcm162-121757.pdf

4 Fricsa, S., Huggins, C., & Unruh, J. (2012). *Land and conflict*. New York: United Nations Interagency Framework Team for Preventive Action. https://www.un.org/en/land-natural-resources-conflict/pdfs/EU-UN%20Introduction%20and%20overview.pdf

5 "About the Sustainable Development Goals – United Nations Sustainable Development." United Nations, United Nations. www.un.org/sustainabledevelopment/sustainable-development-goals/

This house is mine and yet it's not.
The next will also leave this spot.
And when it's passed on to the third,
His soul will fly out like a bird.
One day the fourth will be carried along.
Tell me, to whom does this house belong?
(FOUND ON THE WALL OF AN OLD FARMHOUSE IN GERMANY)

CHAPTER NINE

Material-as-a-Service – rethinking material ownership

If products are offered as a service, consumers no longer become owners: they become users instead. When a service-based contract ends, the materials that make up the product always return to the manufacturer. But what happens when the producer does not need them anymore?

DOI: 10.4324/9781003258674-10

Our family history includes a very special story about German forestry. Thomas's grandparents owned a farm in the Siegerland: a mountainous landscape in mid-western Germany. One of his grandfather's tasks was to lead the so-called Hauberg, or 'clearing mountain' as one could translate it: a cooperative practicing a form of communal forestry management invented in the region during the sixteenth century.

The Siegerland is rich in ore, and mining has been an important activity in the area since as far back as the time of the Kelts (700–200 BC), when the forests were used to produce charcoal for the smelting ovens. By around 200 BC, the once densely wooded mountains had turned into a barren landscape, and the Kelts left the area. It took over 800 years for the area to recover and for people to come back to the mountains. Soon after the Siegerland was repopulated, charcoal production for the mines started to endanger the forests again. This time around, however, the people living in the area became aware of the threat to their existence in time to do something about it. In the sixteenth century, the counts of Nassau and Sayn introduced a new system of forest management: ownership of the forests was to be regulated through cooperatives, in which each forest-owner would receive a share equivalent to the land he owned before. The woodland of each cooperative was divided into 16–20 parcels and each of these parcels was cleared just once every 16–20 years. This way, the forest would have enough time to recover, which secured its existence for generations to come.

This restriction in use did not just save the forest from disappearing again: it also resulted in a transition from a single-cycle monoculture – solely focused on coal burning – to a multi-cyclical, multidimensional way of extracting value from the woodlands. In addition to coal, the production of tanbark and firewood became important, and in addition to forestry, the parcels of land were now used to cultivate rye, buckwheat and wheat during the years just after the timber harvest, followed by communal grazing in the subsequent years.

The Hauberg also had an important social function. A big share of its work could only be done in cooperation, and some of its tasks could only be performed during a few specific days in the year – such as the

peeling of the tanbark, for which the whole community gathered in the forest. In the course of the twentieth century the demand for tanbark and charcoal declined, and most of the area was turned over to high forest management. However, the Hauberg cooperatives still exist today as a cherished part of local culture.

A couple of different aspects of this story fascinate us and makes the story relevant to our future – with respect to material. In the first place, the turn from monoculture to a shifting, multi-cyclical cultivation is significant, as this transformation enabled the creation of multiple values from a limited resource. Secondly, the social cohesion generated by the communal management of the woodlands rendered abuse and destruction almost impossible. Thirdly, the Hauberg is a form of communal and private ownership at the same time: every family has its own share of the cooperatively managed woodland. The responsibilities carried by the community and handed from generation to generation enabled the use as well as the preservation of a limited resource for centuries. The story made us wonder: could we conceive of a way to use *and* preserve material too?

WHO OWNS MATERIAL?

The central question of this book is this: how to organize an economic system that allows current generations to thrive and meet their material needs, while at the same time safeguarding that same material for future generations? In the previous chapters, we have described a number of steps that, if taken, will lead to a situation in which the preservation of material will be prolonged significantly – but we believe that a more fundamental step will still be necessary. However, while the feasibility of all examples in the previous chapters was tested and confirmed by us in real-life projects, the ideas in this chapter are more of a thought experiment; they might be even received as provocative. We therefore ask our distinguished readers to bear with us during a little intellectual adventure.

When looking at material from an intergenerational perspective the question arises: who owns material? Borrowing from the ideas of the famous Swiss watchmaker Patek Philippe, we dare to proclaim: "one never actually owns material – one merely takes care of it for the next generation." This idea is generally accepted for Swiss watches and other valuable family property: we are allowed to use it, provided we preserve its utility for the next generation. This implies, that in fact we are – at least mentally – replacing *ownership* with the right to *use*. This is also what happened in the Hauberg.

It is not our intention to propose the abolishment of private property, but we believe that we should learn from the ownership of financially or emotionally valuable objects to expand the way we treat and preserve them to include *all* the materials we use in our daily life. Many of the products made of these materials have no sentimental value: we certainly would not consider to pass our washing machines, TVs or blenders on to our grandchildren. Yet the material they are made of certainly has to be preserved for their generation, which makes it more sensible to organize the use of these products in the form of service models, rather than in the form of irresponsible ownership. This, however, is something we cannot do on our own – even individual companies would probably not be able to safeguard material for generations to come: we need to organize this collectively.

GOVERNING THE COMMONS OF OUR LIMITED SYSTEM

"There is a clear increase in attention for the kind of arrangements in which people collectively take responsibility for the common resources needed to sustain both their lifestyle and their environment," the Dutch philosopher Hans Achterhuis wrote in 2010.[1] For decades, the idea of the commonality had suffered from a bad reputation. In addition to the images evoked by economies in the former Soviet States – in which a heavy governmental structure suffocated all individual entrepreneurial spirit – the merit of the commons seemed discredited once and for all by a famous academic publication. In 1968, *Science Magazine* – one of the world's top academic journals – published *The Tragedy of the Commons*:[2] an article by the Californian ecologist Garrett Hardin, in which he sketched the following scenario:

"Picture a pasture open to all," he wrote.

> It is to be expected that each herdsman will try to keep as many cattle as possible on the commons. Such an arrangement may work reasonably satisfactorily for centuries, because tribal wars and disease keep the numbers of both man and beast well below the carrying capacity of the land. Finally, however, comes the day of reckoning. That is, the day when the long-desired goal of social stability becomes a reality. At this point, the inherent logic of the commons remorselessly generates tragedy.

He goes on to explain a theory that since has become famous in the world of economics, social psychology and game theory.

This 'Tragedy of the Commons' allegedly arises when a group of individuals collectively make use of a common pool resource: from the fish in the ocean to the food in an office fridge. After the publication of Hardin's paper, its title quickly became a famous catchphrase – and if catchy metaphors are popular in general, they are especially irresistible in the complex world of economics. There is a kind of aesthetic elegance to simple theories describing complex situations, and they can be understood by anyone. This makes them politically useful, but no means always correct.

It was another American scientist who started the rehabilitation of the commons. Elinor Ostrom, the first woman ever to win the Nobel Prize for Economics in 2009, refuted the assumption that underlies our current political and economic paradigm: the idea of the modern human as a *homo economicus* – completely blinded by self-interest. When watching Garrets lecture in 1968 she was electrified, not because she agreed with him, but because she was convinced he was wrong. Ostrom's findings during years of research convinced her of a view of human beings as capable of collaborating for the greater good, and of regarding the interests of the community as equally or even more important than their immediate self-interest. Her extensive research centered on the governance of common pool resources in various places.

Through intensive fieldwork, Ostrom discovered a reality that was much more complex and multidimensional than any of the theoretical models so loved by economists and political scientists would have her believe. She discovered a number of design principles that enable communities to successfully govern a common resource, without generating any kind of tragedy. She found that common pool resources are only overexploited in situations in which there exist no collective responsibility, rules or transparency with regard to the utilization of these resources. Most importantly, she discovered that common resource management is in fact very well-suited to regulating the use of a limited resource that also needs to be preserved for future generations – and that such collective management of resources can exist *within the context of a capitalist society.*[3]

Ostrom absolutely saw a parallel in the overexploitation of global resources and Hardy's famous pasture. However, precisely because of the fact that these resources in today's world are not treated as common property, we cannot really speak of a tragedy of the commons – rather, we should speak of the tragedy of no-man's land.

That brings us back to a point we made earlier, which is that the separation of power and responsibility is the fundamental problem of our current economic system. The big question therefore is how to reunite power and responsibility: what design principles and governance structures do we need, in order to manage the limited material resources in our system collectively and responsibly? How can we organize the ownership of material in such a way that it will be possible for material both to be utilized in the present *and* to be preserved for future generations?

The model we will propose here has been designed to lead to a new value chain, via a number of consecutive steps. All of these steps constitute building blocks, which taken together can form a system that facilitates material preservation and eliminates waste.

THE TURNTOO MODEL

STEP 1: PRODUCT-AS-A-SERVICE – PERMANENT PRODUCER RESPONSIBILITY

When products turn into services, manufacturers will start taking responsibility for the entire life cycle of a product, while consumers will just pay for the right to use the product for a fixed period of time. During this period of time, the manufacturer remains responsible for the performance of the product, as well as for repairs and potential upgrades.

STEP 2: PRODUCT AS A MATERIAL DEPOT – MODULAR DESIGN AND ASSEMBLY

Upon termination of the contract, the product returns to the manufacturer. The producer will then be able to either offer the product to a different kind of consumer, transform it, reuse the materials used for its production for an entirely different purpose or sell those materials to a different manufacturer. That requires that the manufacturer has designed and manufactured the product as a material depot: the product and all its components must be fully modular and must have lost none of its reusability on a material level.

STEP 3: MATERIAL PASSPORT

Due to the fact that the product potentially will be used over a longer period of time, information about materials used must be documented in a material passport. In this material passport, producers will document the exact combination of materials and resources used for the production of a given product or building.

STEP 4: MADASTER

By registering the material passport in the Madaster archive, the preservation of the materials will be guaranteed, independent of the producer's continued existence. The registration of the materials creates transparency about their location, financial value and their individual possibilities regarding reuse. The standardization of information makes it possible to share information and form marketplaces for secondary material.

STEP 5: THE UNIVERSAL DECLARATION OF MATERIAL RIGHTS

The Universal Declaration of Material Rights, in the meantime, protects the rights of those individual materials and resources – so that they retain the right to identity and utility at all times, even if, for some reason, their material passport has been lost.

This way, we will have taken five steps in the direction of an economic model in which the loss of material can be prevented. Still, these steps only address the tail end of the existing linear chain. By adopting them, we will break out of the linear one-dimensional perspective of our current system, but one important question remains: what happens to materials when (for whatever reason) a producer does not need or want them anymore and finds himself unable to sell them to another producer? If we don't find an answer to this question, materials will still be at risk of getting lost. Another problem, meanwhile, is the possible rise of resource monopolies: dominant manufacturers could start 'hoarding' resources and materials, disrupting the balance of the market. To prevent these things from happening, we will have to reorganize the supply chain even more radically. We, therefore, believe it is time to stop trying to fix the system in a backward direction – and start forging agreements on the conditions for the use of material right from the beginning of the chain. Ultimately, we are in need of an entirely new architecture for the supply chain we depend on: one in which resources can circulate forever.

STEP 6: MATERIAL-AS-A-SERVICE

In order to design this step, we will have to rethink our current notions of ownership, and how we can facilitate the use of material in the present while safeguarding it for future generations at the same time. We believe that the Hauberg example can help us find a model in which material can be used without transferring all the rights connected to ownership. The classic definition of ownership rights defines four different civilian property interests:

1 The right to use or enjoy a thing possessed, directly and without altering it (Use).
2 The right to derive profit from a thing possessed: for instance, by selling crops, leasing immovables or annexed movables, taxing for entry and so on (Usufruct).
3 The right to alienate the thing possessed, either by consuming or destroying it (e.g., for profit).
4 The right of transferring the property to someone else (e.g., sale, exchange, and gift).

These four different interests can also be divided between different parties; while one party is the owner of the thing, it can transfer the right of use or usufruct to someone else.

Looking at the big picture makes it clear that we will need an intergenerational treaty regarding the ownership of resources (property right four). Present generations will have to act as custodians of our shared resources, and will only be entitled to exercise the first two rights by using the material and or derive profit from its exploitation. The application of the third interest – as the right to transform material into waste – cannot be sustained from this perspective. Interestingly, the official Latin name of this property right is *abusus*, the literal application of 'abusus' to our natural resources has become a direct threat to the future of our planet.

Therefore, we will have to rethink the entire value chain, which in its present form amounts to a value destruction chain. The way we envision this is by connecting the right to process material to conditions based upon use, not consumption: on *usus*, not *abusus*.

Instead of acquiring all four property rights, which come along with ownership, the consumer – or user – will only pay for the right to use a product. The manufacturer, in turn, will only acquire the right of usufruct. This right of usufruct will be passed along the value chain, along with the contractual obligation that requires the material to be preserved and its usability permanently guaranteed. Like consumers, producers too will no longer acquire the ownership of materials. They will still *use* materials to make their products, of course, but the ownership of materials and resources will stay with a single party: the Earth.

How do we do that? By fundamentally reorganizing the whole value chain, basing *every* agreement, from mine to consumer, on the model of *usus* instead of *abusus*. This means that even mines will have to stop selling materials and resources, and start offering them as a service to producers, in the way that producers offer their products as services to their consumers in the *Product-as-a-Service* business model. A second model will thus arise: *Material-as-a-Service*, based on the fact that not only products and buildings can be seen as resource depots: the ultimate resource depot is, of course, our planet Earth. Producers will just hold the resources and materials in trust, without owning them – in a modern, worldwide version of common pool resource management.

To guarantee that resources remain valuable to each actor in the supply chain, conditions concerning their treatment must be legally agreed upon in a contract *before* they enter the chain. Every actor in the chain will then bestow upon the next a *concession on the condition of preservation*.

This means that extracted resources will never be sold: they will merely be provided as a service. Purchasers of *resource use* can resell the right to the use of that resource for as long as they want, on the condition that the material, as soon as it is no longer needed, will be returned to wherever it came from (step 6). UDMR will further see to it that materials keep their utility, and guarantee that they will be treated with respect at all times (step 5). The identity and location of the materials are documented in a Material Passport and registered in Madaster (step 3 and 4), and the product in which the materials are processed is designed as a material depot (step 2) and can only be offered to consumers as a service (step 1).

This way, we will always know which materials have been used, where they are located and where they came from. Every time a material shifts in the chain, whether backward or forward, an entry or exit stamp will be added to its passport, so that the information is always up to date. Registration of material locations will become comparable to a visa documenting your stay in a foreign country.

What is important is that it is guaranteed that the protection we normally derive from ownership (protection that ensures us that it will be worth our while to invest in something like building a house or manufacturing a product) will be provided by generally agreed upon terms. If producers are allowed to hold materials and resources for as long as they need them, they will be assured of the fact that these products – in which they have invested time, money and labor – cannot be taken from them – even if they do not own the materials they are made of. They will, however, need to account for these materials with regard to the party in the chain before them. The right to use the material is acquired together with the contractual obligation to permanently preserve the material and ensure its usability. Variations in the length of time producers will want to use (and thus hold) the materials used are dependent on the context: a product's segment or target audience, the materials used, and the business model employed.

A commonly agreed upon arrangement like the one we are proposing is not just important for the actors who are directly involved in it. If ownership of materials and resources always stays with community or the state in which they were mined, it will be important for every person on Earth that every actor in the chain has the right to use materials for as long as they need them. That way, people and companies at every stage in the chain will be ensured that it will be worthwhile to add value to the resource, material or service, by investing time, money and labor – all the way from the mine to the manufactured product.

Consumers will thus be provided with all sorts of products they cannot or do not want to produce themselves, and each separate actor in the chain will make a profit. Companies at every stage in the chain will benefit from decreased material cost, since they will no longer have to purchase the material – but acquire only the right to use it.

THE ETERNAL CHAIN

The chain, in the meantime, will now start and end with planet Earth, in the form of the mine. It will consist of the traditional *value creation chain*, which reaches from the raw material to the manufactured product. From this point, there will be a new part of the chain, which we defined as *value preservation chain*, which starts at the product and goes back to the raw material.

We believe that the idea of Material-as-a-Service may form an indispensable ingredient of a truly all-encompassing Harvest Society. Value creation and value preservation, the two parts of the Turntoo-model (as shown on page X), together form an eternal chain in which value is added in the forward direction, and preserved in the backwards direction.

The process of *value creation* starts at the mine. The mandate to monetize natural resources remains with community or the state playing the role of the steward of the materials found within its territory. This entity provides the mining company with a concession for the extraction of raw materials and the right to pass on its right to hold on to the material to other companies, who, in turn, will process the materials into intermediate products. Those companies then provide manufacturers with concessions to use and process the materials into the components needed to assemble retail products, and provide other manufacturers with a concession to do so. Finally, consumers will make use of these products via service contracts. When these contracts end, the products are returned to the manufacturer in the form of a depot of components, materials

TURNTO

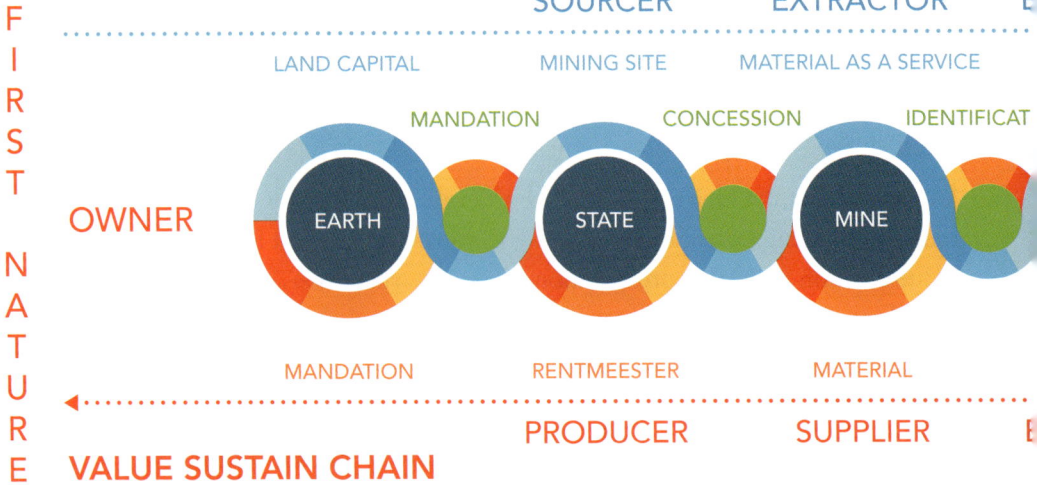

FIRST NATURE

SOURCER — LAND CAPITAL — MINING SITE — MATERIAL AS A SERVICE — EXTRACTOR

MANDATION — CONCESSION — IDENTIFICAT

OWNER — EARTH — STATE — MINE

MANDATION — RENTMEESTER — MATERIAL

PRODUCER — SUPPLIER

VALUE SUSTAIN CHAIN

PERPETUAL M

- MODEL

VALUE CREATION CHAIN

SECOND NATURE

| GER | SUPPLIER | PRODUCER | |
| COMPONENTS | PRODUCT | PRODUCT AS A SERVICE |

PERMISSION   PASSPORT   VISA

SUPPLIER   PRODUCER   USER   USER

MATERIALS DEPOT   COMPONENT DEPOT   PRODUCT AS A DEPOT

GER   EXTRACTOR   SOURCER

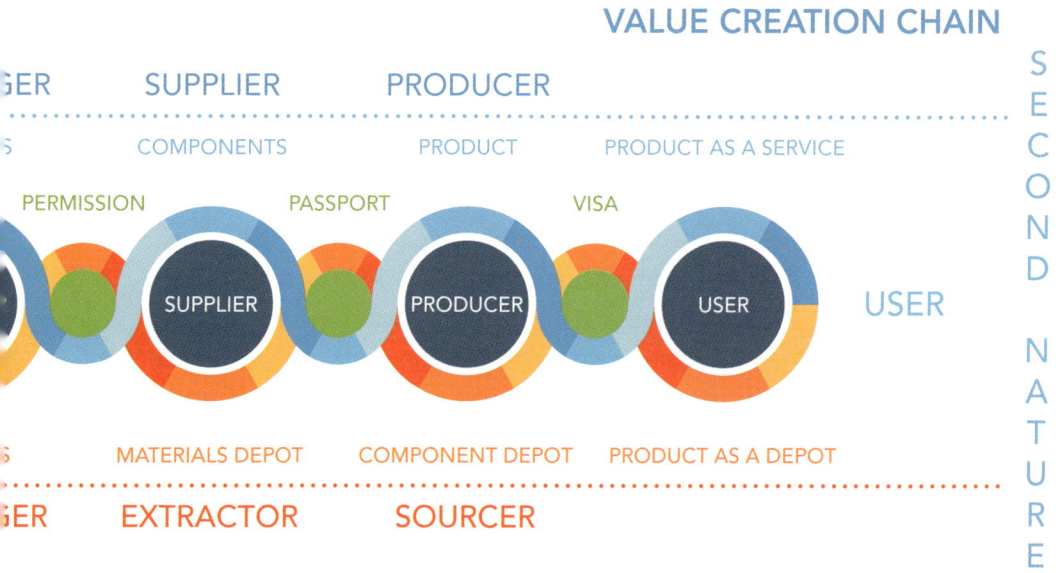

ERIAL CHAIN

turn too

and resources – documented in a Material Passport. This is where the backward chain of *value preservation* starts.

Materials and products can continue to circulate because of certain conditions governing the chain: concessions are only provided on the condition of preservation and precise documentation. Production processes and systems, as well as the products themselves, are designed to facilitate the preservation of value, enabling materials to remain undamaged as they travel backwards in the chain. Every phase of the supply chain will start with the establishment of a mutual agreement regarding the terms of return. The way anything moves forward in the chain will be determined by the way it will be able to move backward in the future.

This will give rise to a chain of circles, in which materials move around. The *Product-as-a-Service* business model (right part of the graph on page 187) ensures that products return to producers after use, but when a producer decides to change his production process, he will be able to return the components of his current products back to the circle preceding his own. When that happens, the material shifts one circle backward: from the retail manufacturer's circle to the product component manufacturer's circle. The latter can then determine whether they want to find other manufacturers in need of these components, or whether they will likewise return the components to the next circle backward in the chain, to the manufacturers of intermediate products, and via them possibly all the way back to the mine – the last and first link in the Turntoo model. This last step is just a theoretical one, however; in practice, we expect resources to circulate forever.

RIGHT OF USE AND THE PERMANENT MATERIAL FUND

As long as the material circulates, a continuous source of income is generated for the place the material came from. All actors in the chain, after all, keep on paying for the right to hold on to the material for as long as they use it. This way, the state or community benefits from the value creation realized by providing its raw materials to the global economy.

An example of such a system, at least partially, can be found in the Alaska Permanent Fund, which was set up in 1976 in order to invest at least 25% of the income generated from the oil extracted in the area into a dedicated fund for future generations, who would no longer have oil as a resource. In addition, all Alaskan residents are entitled to a yearly payment: the Alaska Permanent Dividend. Admittedly, oil is not be a very good example in the context of this book, but what we find interesting is the idea of a permanent capital flow to the inhabitants of the area and a provision for future generations.[4]

Let's imagine, for example, a resource rich area in Africa. Instead of selling the rights to mine a certain resource to a foreign mining company, the state or community only gives out a license to the mining company – which allows them to extract the material and sell the right of usufruct to users. A part of the generated income will go to the mining company for its work, while another part will go to the community in which area the resource was mined – which now will benefit from continuous value creation through the resources extracted from its territory.

This also has a significant social impact: instead of a system based on overexploitation and destruction of resources, the system will distribute the creation of wealth more equally. Local communities in resource-rich, often less developed countries would grant the usufruct of materials mined on their territory and receive a continuous remuneration in return. The governance for this system would involve increased interdependence and cooperation, which we believe would be an additional stabilizing factor in global relations.

GOVERNING THE MATERIAL COMMONS

We also expect that, when it comes to the registration of products, and most likely also when it comes to the trade in the right to use them, institutions will be needed to bridge the gap between the companies extracting resources on the one hand, and the companies refining and processing them on the other (what we call the *exchanger* in our model). We have already founded one of these institutions ourselves: the Madaster foundation, which we described in Chapter 6. Technology will thereby be an important enabler to create the transparency needed to manage complex material streams. Technologies such as blockchain and AI will undoubtedly enable us to track and trace material through a complex global system.

In the transition to this new model, roles will shift and give rise to new ones. We will have to figure out collectively how to distribute these. In this respect, we would like to refer to what Elinor Ostrom called a polycentric design of governance structures for common pool resources, complex structures and binding agreements between different parties directly involved in the exploitation of a specific resource. We envision neither centralized state-controlled systems nor privately owned monopolistic structures to shape this new system. Instead, we expect that many different structures and initiatives will emerge that will manage many different chains of value preservation, because though so far we have spoken about a single chain, the reality is much more complex and will consist of many different of these chains. The Hauberg cooperative story, as well as many of Elinor Ostrom's research findings, tells us that there are many ways of organizing collective resource management – including many that are more horizontal than top-down. The important thing is that we need to find a way to work together and ensure that the power to take decisions and the responsibility to deal with the consequences are no longer separated.

Another important aspect is the respect for current property rights in the transition to a Material-as-a-Service system. The example of the Hauberg might be inspirational, in that case: entitlements to a specific area of land were translated into shares in the new entities created, which fully paid tribute to the old ownership structure and yet allowed the creation of the new future proof system. The number of 'Pennigs' owned by Haubergowners today still represents the size of the property his forefathers once owned in the forests of the Siegerland. Yet at the same time, it is obvious that not all material needs to be managed as a service. Important is that there will be a distinction between material used for temporary applications and material used in products, which will be handed from generation to generation anyway. Nobody would want to pay a monthly service fee for his or her wedding ring.

The Turntoo-model described above is capable of making sure that resources and materials will remain accessible. It satisfies the condition that we must end the production process with the same set of resources as the one we started it with. Nothing would get lost in this economic system, and nothing would prevent us from reusing resources again and again. Create, sustain and secure: that is the essence of the model.

The advantages are clear. First and foremost the sustained existence of the Earth's resources: source of all life. Waste will become a concept of the past, because material will always be treated as a resource. The service contract guarantees the return first of products and eventually of the materials they were made of; some after a short period of time, others after years of use. No matter how long it takes for products and materials to return; however, the moment will always have been anticipated: it will have been determined beforehand, and documented in the service contract. This way, manufacturers will gain control over the management of their own resource supply – and independence from the supply problems and price insecurities we mentioned earlier. In addition, they will enjoy regular, predictable incomes, in the form of continuous cash flows. They will thus enjoy more stability, and they will be exposed to much fewer risks. And *last but not least*: consumers will no longer be burdened with products that are designed to break, or responsibilities they are unable to oversee.

STEWARDS

Even though, in the new model, we will not strictly be 'owners' but temporary 'users,' we will still need to deal with the responsibilities normally associated with ownership. Each actor in the chain must be held accountable for the following of rules and terms agreed upon in service contracts. 'Possession' in the new economy will not refer to ownership but to good *stewardship*, which is about taking responsibilities. Stewardship is not about 'having' things, but about taking care of things. In our *Product-as-a-Service* contracts, for instance, we have included the 'prudence principle': consumers need to be committed to treating products with care – if they fail to do so, manufacturers will be able to hold them responsible.

We are often confronted with the argument that a circular economy is impossible to realize because of wear and tear and potential loss, which is natural to every item made of physical matter. While we definitely acknowledge that these have to be factored in one way or another in this new model, our counter argument would be that no-one would ever consider to stop feeding a baby only because he knows that this human being will die anyway in the course of his of her life. On the contrary, knowing about the vulnerability of the human life, we take every precaution possible to protect it. The Turntoo model also has the potential to change the way consumers treat products – further prolonging their life cycles – by making them see products for what they really are: conglomerates of finite resources and materials within a closed system, serving a temporary need. This way, we can all accept our responsibility toward our planet and all the generations of people that will come after we have gone, while still enjoying everything our Earth has to offer us – conscious of the fact that humanity is dependent on Nature and that our presence may be temporary, but the consequences of our actions permanent.

The advantages of our system are manifold:

1 It establishes a respectful relationship between humanity and the planet.
2 Material is protected from being turned into waste by binding agreements between the parties in the new value chain.
3 There will be a continuous flow of capital from resource intensive industrialized countries, enabling resource-rich but less

industrialized countries to benefit from the value creation made possible by the materials mined on their territory.

4 A service agreement defines the return of materials and products, enabling manufacturers to manage the installed base of products at their clients as a material depot. This lowers the risk in their supply chains regarding the supply of resources or price volatilities.

5 The system will also change the financial model of companies – instead of one-off sales, the service model will create a recurring revenue stream for manufacturers, which results in greater financial stability and long-term customer relationships.

6 Users will have access to high-quality products, which will no longer be designed for obsolescence, but for longevity and upgrades. In addition, they will be relieved from a burden they were never capable of bearing anyway: the responsibility for the disposal of products and the preservation of the material they contain.

7 The model might also contribute to increased stability and peaceful international relations. An economic system, which through cooperation and mutual dependencies on many levels enables a fairer distribution of global wealth, can contribute to lowering geopolitical tensions. For this reason, we were invited to present UDMR at the Carnegie Peacebuilding Conversations in the Peace Palace in The Hague.

8 Admittedly, the ideas presented here are far-reaching, and their implementation will require a fundamental change of consciousness and increased cooperation between many different players in the global economy. The question of the organization of the Material-as-a-Service model is still to be explored: it we will require many new rules and procedures, which we as human beings will have to cocreate. Yet we will have to develop new forms of cooperation either way, if we want to make the necessary transition to a future-proof economic system.

The organization of cooperation was the central theme under which the Nobel Prize for Elinor Ostrom was awarded: we could not agree more, this would not only lead to a completely new economic system, it would lead to a new culture, one in which we have changed the soul of the economy.

NOTES

1 Achterhuis, H. (2010) *De utopie van de vrije markt*. Rotterdam: Lemniscaat.

2 Hardin, G. (1968). "The tragedy of the commons." *Science*, Vol. 162, pp. 1243–1248.

3 Ostrom, E. (2015). *Governing the commons: The evolution of institutions for collective action* (Canto Classics). Cambridge: Cambridge University Press. doi:10.1017/CBO9781316423936

4 Alaska Permanent Fund Corporation. https://apfc.org/

We are only travelers in this world, not inhabitants.
(ERASMUS OF ROTTERDAM)

CHAPTER TEN

Completing the Copernican revolution

We know that our Earth is a fragile ecosystem in an enormous universe – and that it is by no means at its center. We also know that as human beings, we are part of Nature. But our culture still reflects a different worldview: the idea of our planet as a machine and man as ruler of Nature. How can we recalibrate our relationship with our environment?

DOI: 10.4324/9781003258674-11

At 17:32 on December 24, 1968, the first-ever photo of planet Earth was taken from aboard the Apollo 8 spacecraft. Three days earlier, this first manned mission to be put in orbit around the moon had left our planet with three astronauts on board. Among whom was James Lovell, who would later be a member of the Apollo 13 crew.

Lovell and his colleagues were the first humans ever to see the Earth from this unprecedented point of view: surrounded by inscrutable pitch-black space, it 'rose' above the horizon of the moon's gray crater landscape.[1]

Strangely enough, no one had anticipated this moment, and taking a photo of it was not part of the NASA script: it was a spontaneous and unauthorized impulse on the part of astronaut William Anders that gave us this historic image in black and white. The crew was overwhelmed and called for authorization by NASA to use a color film.

The photo, which became famous under the title *Earthrise*, changed the way we view our planet forever. For the first time in history, we beheld the vulnerability and limitations of the place we call home: a momentous event in the relationship between humans and the Earth. It was this documentation that led to the founding of many environmental organizations all over the world: organizations like Friends of the Earth, the Natural Resources Defense Council and Greenpeace. 1970 is widely considered to be the year the modern environmental movement was born. Governments also started to act: the EPA was founded by President Nixon in 1970, and the first-ever 'Earth Day' was celebrated the same year.[2] In Europe, the 1970 European Nature Conservation Year was celebrated: the first Europe-wide environmental campaign, incorporating over 200,000 individual projects.

Of course, even before 1970, there had been plenty of pioneers – Rachel Carsson's famous book Silent Spring was published in 1962, and historians like Joachim Radkau date the beginning of today's environmental movement all the way back to the debate surrounding wood shortages in 1800. But environmentalists had never before been

NICOLAI
COPERNICI TO-
RINENSIS DE REVOLVTIONI-
bus orbium coelestium,
Libri VI.

IN QVIBVS STELLARVM ET FI-
XARVM ET ERRATICARVM MOTVS, EX VETE-
ribus atq̃ recentibus obseruationibus, reſtituit hic autor.
Præterea tabulas expeditas luculentasq̃ addidit, ex qui-
bus eosdem motus ad quoduis tempus Mathe-
matum ſtudioſus facillime calcu-
lare poterit.

ITEM, DE LIBRIS REVOLVTIONVM NICOLAI
Copernici Narratio prima, per M. Georgium Ioachi-
mum Rheticum ad D. Ioan. Schone-
rum ſcripta.

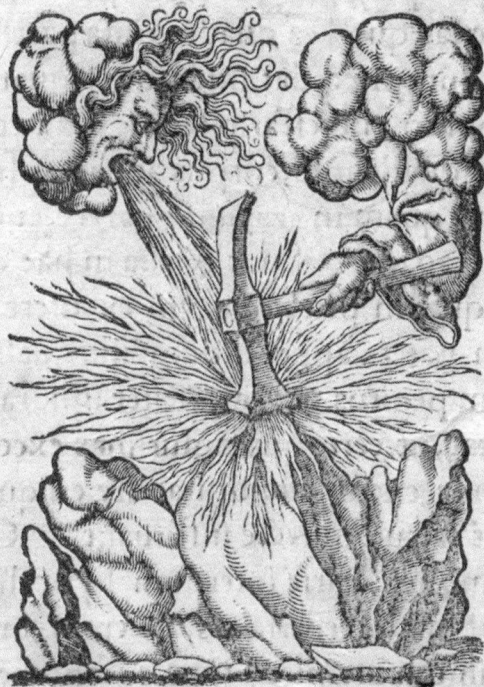

Cum Gratia & Priuilegio Cæſ. Maieſt.

BASILEAE, EX OFFICINA
HENRICPETRINA.

united into a movement of this scale – nor had their views ever received this much attention.

In a way, the image functioned as a long overdue visual support for a shift in our thinking that had started with the Prussian astronomer Nicolaus Copernicus. He was one of the first people to put forward, in 1543, the idea that the sun forms the center of a solar system – and that the rest of the planets in this system circle around it: a conception of the universe that has become known as the *helio*centric worldview.[3] Until the mid-sixteenth century, people believed the Earth to form the center of the universe – and this *geo*centric worldview was never questioned.

When around 1610 the telescope was invented, Galileo Galilei was able to study planetary movements and found proof of Copernicus's hypothesis based on his observations of Venus. These observations brought Galilei into a serious conflict with the Roman church. Within the church, people did not want to hear of a worldview in which the Earth (and its humans with it) was anything less than the central point of God's creation. While the church usually kept its distance from scientific debates, in this case, it decided to call Galilei to account. Galilei – a devout Catholic himself – however, was of the opinion that his findings did not contradict Catholic doctrine at all; he thought they merely showed how well thought-out God's creation was. Twice, the church sent the Inquisition to investigate Galilei's scientific works. In 1616, he received a warning not to support the Copernican system – but despite this warning, Galileo published his famous book *Dialogo sopra i due massimi sistemi del mondo* (Dialogue Concerning the Two Chief World Systems)[4] for which he eventually was sentenced to a life-long house arrest in 1633. Upon hearing this verdict, it is rumored, he proclaimed "Eppur si muove!" (and still she moves!).

Fifty years later, Isaac Newton would build onto Galilei's theory and receive wide acclaim, but it wasn't until 1992 that the Roman church acknowledged Galileo Galilei's scientific contribution officially. "Life is understood backwards, but it has to be lived forwards" as the Danish philosopher Soren Kierkegaard once wrote in his diary. In other words: 'reality' can often only be perceived in hindsight.[5]

CROWN OF CREATION?

Nowadays, the term 'Copernican revolution' or 'Copernican shift' is used to indicate a radical reorientation in science or philosophy, which makes us perceive reality in the light of a completely different conceptual framework – comparable to the shift in our thinking caused by Copernicus's discovery. Looking at our current cultural paradigm, however, we believe that as much as the original Copernican shift has changed the way we rationally *think*, it has never penetrated any of the other dimensions a cultural paradigm consists of: feeling, expression and action. The Copernican shift, therefore, is anything but complete.

Looking at our actions, stories and attitudes, it would soon become clear to any outside observer that we still do not fully realize what our place in this universe is: that we are by no means at its center – neither in location nor importance.

However, we think we might currently find ourselves on the eve of the completion of this shift. Not led by scientific discovery or increasing technological possibilities, this time, but by grim necessity. Not *possibilities*, but *necessities* will soon start dictating change, as a matter of fact, they already start doing so and we simply cannot afford to understand reality until after the event, at this point: there is far too much at stake. Our timing, therefore, is essential: we must change the very soul of our culture and economic system – and quickly.

Our economic culture, as we know it today, mirrors the old geocentric worldview as well as another view that has historically been closely linked to the idea of the Earth as the center of the universe: the idea of humans as the crown of creation. Influenced by thousands of years of Western philosophy, starting with Plato's Theory of Forms and centuries long reinforced by (mainly) Christianity, we have been subconsciously permeated by ideas that regard our Earthly lives as second-rate, and the carnal, the concrete, the *natural* as something to transcend.

In the late Middle Ages and Renaissance, this division has been culturally magnified by the Inquisition, which deemed 'pagan' everything natural, and regarded the subjugation of Nature as our Divine Mission (Genesis 1). This last imagine probably arose from a specific translation of the Bible, in which the original Hebrew text, which could be interpreted as "the mission of mankind to take care of the Earth like a good shepherd" was translated into a mandate to dominate our world.

Ever since the time of the Enlightenment, this worldview has been mixed with a dogmatic belief in science as our ultimate savior. The famous French philosopher Descartes did not just write the culturally defining sentence "I think, therefore I am" in his *Discours de la méthode* in 1637. Less famously, but no less influential, he wrote that science would turn humans into "*maîtres et possesseurs de la Nature*" (rulers and owners of Nature).[6] And while our society may have been largely secularized, these part-religious ideas still function as the foundations of our worldview. They find new forms, ones that fit into the new paradigm of scientism: the inexhaustible belief in the human 'manufacturability' of the world via the natural sciences and technological innovation. The developments of the past few centuries seemed to underwrite and validate this view: an explosion of scientific discovery and an impressive parade of technological inventions have brought us a standard of living that is historically unprecedented, changing our society faster than ever before. By now, however, there is no denying that this worldview and the culture it produces has a downside: the ecological crisis it causes threatens to put everything we have achieved in serious danger. The exploitation and pollution that are damaging our Earth are the direct results of a philosophical viewpoint that lies at the very roots of our culture.

LINEAR CULTURE

As we've described above, our world is shaped by the consciousness through which it is perceived – but that proposition works the other way, too. The world in which we grow up and the logic that dictates its rules determine the way we perceive our world.

The linear economy we've discussed so extensively has arisen from the worldview and culture described above – but it produces a 'linear culture' in turn: a culture of manufacturability, focused on the achievement of quantitative results, and a social world governed by the idea that *only that which we can measure has truth,* and *only that which we can count has value.* This linear motto can be found in almost anything: our priorities, the way we 'handle' problems, the way we evaluate situations and the way we treat each other and our planet.

We prefer to cut the world up in small, manageable, isolated pieces: modeled after the way we have cut up our production processes ever since the time of the Industrial Revolution. We don't do this without reason: in the case of manufacturing, this method has made the process vastly more efficient, leading to the levels of wealth, we see around us today. When each link in the chain focuses on a single aspect of production, the entire process (assisted by automation) can suddenly be executed countless times faster than before, when a single craftsman or craftswoman would have to acquire the skills needed for each part of the procedure and perform each of its steps on their own. Linear thinking, therefore, is obviously not without merit: it can be incredibly functional. Still, a lot is lost or destroyed and a lot of valuable things escape our perception if the linear perspective is our only one.

In the academic world, too, the linear tradition of compartmentalizing and artificially isolating subjects has taken a strong hold. Scientists focus on precisely defined fields, carefully separated from the rest of the world. The idea behind this method is that we will eventually understand the world at large if each person focuses on one small part of the puzzle, as all those pieces put together will show us 'the big picture.'

That idea presupposes an image of the world as a machine; however, all of the components of which can be taken apart and understood separately – without their losing their function and value in relation to each other and the contraption as a whole. Unfortunately, this image ignores something vital: our planet is not a machine. It is a living ecosystem in which everything is connected – and everything important. The world cannot be understood as a simple combination of puzzle pieces: it's characterized by a complexity that we will never fully grasp. The seams in the fabric are mere fabrications of our own mind, ways to comprehend the endlessly complex world around us. They function as the grid through which we can look at the world without getting dizzy.

Today, the influence of our actions has become so enormous that most of them have global impact. We travel the world and import our food and clothes from all over the planet. Climate problems or nuclear disasters are by no means 'contained' by national borders, nor is their effect confined to only one dimension. Climate change, migration, resource security, peace: all our global challenges are closely interrelated. Everything influences everything else, after all.

Compartmentalizing the world, whether into links in a supply chain, isolated scientific subjects or national territories, results in losing the overall view – while that is exactly the perspective we need if we want to stand a chance of overcoming the problems we are currently facing. Our complex, interconnected world will simply never answer to a one-dimensional, linear way of thinking. The linear culture, therefore, is the paradigm we ought to rid ourselves of. We may build onto the amazing things achieved through this linear focus, but the time has come to broaden our perspective and infuse our culture with that which comes into view. Our Earth is a living, rhythmic, cyclical system – and it is time to start treating it as such.

In order to change our own relationship with our planet at large, we will therefore have to adapt to a new system of economics, but in order to get to that system, we will first have to profoundly change our cultural view of it. We must change the very soul of our cultural and economic world.

CHRONOS AND KAIROS

Greek mythology features Chronos, symbolizing linear time, and Kairos, representing opportunity: the exact right moment to do something. Chronos is quantitative, the time of the clock, whereas Kairos stands for quality: ripeness, timing. In our self-created world, Chronos has become an overpowering tyrant: our schedules rule our lives, we continuously keep an eye on the clock and we are woken up by the mechanical beepings of our alarm clocks every morning. Everything is approached and organized *chronologically* – linear. The right moment to do something thus becomes nothing more than the moment scheduled for it.

Even our own biographical development is mostly regarded in a linear way: careers must follow straight lines, preferably avoiding any wanderings or failures; the development of our children is standardized and closely followed in diagrams, precise lines unblemished by even the smallest deviations.

The way in which our society dismisses the elderly, too, allows for a comparison to our linear throwaway economy: we mindlessly destroy immense wealth in the form of wisdom, knowledge and life experience, which for good reasons is highly valued in most other cultures.

"Everything in life is growth. Not numbering and counting, but ripening like a tree, which doesn't force its sap and stands confidently in the storms of spring, knowing that summer will come eventually," the poet Rainer Maria Rilke once wrote in a famous letter to the young aspiring poet Franz Kappus. His analogy to Nature was no coincidence: Nature's development does not just follow Chronos – Kairos is at least as important to it. To the ancient Greeks, Chronos represented the eternal time, the exchanging of night for day, the movement of the stars and the eternal return of the seasons. In music, he would be time and rhythm – the regularity in everything. However, time and rhythm alone do not yet constitute a musical composition.

That which turns a rhythm into a piece of music is a melody, which is what Kairos represents. The wind and the weather are not ruled by regularity: they play their melody on the rhythm set by the sun, but they are not controlled by it. A fruit falls from the tree when it's ripe – no sooner, no later.

regularity: they play their melody on the rhythm set by the sun, but they are not controlled by it. A fruit falls from the tree when it's ripe – no sooner, no later.

Everything that is alive is governed by an internal rhythm, and no two rhythms are exactly the same. This applies to each part and process of our closed system, including ourselves. We lose our milk teeth when we're about 7 years old, we become sexually mature around the age of 14, and as of our 21st birthday, we may regard ourselves as fully grown up. Those transition periods usually aren't very comfortable. On the contrary, more often than not they are highly uncomfortable. They cannot be skipped, however. The precise rhythm, as we mentioned already, differs from person to person, depending on a sheer infinite number of variables.

The melody of even a single life, therefore, is infinitely variable – influenced by an intricacy of forces far beyond our comprehension, it can change its tune at any given moment. Our forced attempts to replace Kairos with Chronos, therefore, brings us into conflict with (our) Nature, whose laws we will never be able to escape – in spite of our most detailed Excel sheets, plans and alarm clocks.

Sitting in our heated, atmospherically lit living rooms, whose climates and lighting are entirely under our control, we feel like we are the rulers of the universe. Protected by four strong walls and a ceiling, we are enchanted by this 'second Nature' of our own design – which outside takes the shape of cars, apartment buildings, highways, bridges and neatly raked front yards. This illusion is so powerful that we have started believing more in our human-made world than in the overarching natural world of which we ourselves are but a product. No one, however, can produce a snowdrop, manufacture a living tree or transcend the laws of Nature. When a heavy storm tears a weighty branch off the old oak tree in our garden, causing it to land on our roof, a heavy bang and its resulting damage will remind us of our place on Earth.

We never really escape the merciless natural world. Each one of us is as vulnerable as every other part of our interconnected system. Indeed, our 'second Nature' has never transcended that natural world at all – and it will only have a future if it is developed according to Nature's regularities and laws. When we realize that humans will never be able to place themselves or their actions outside of the natural world, we must accept that we are by no means this world's central concern. Despite the increasingly destructive power of humans, *Nature* is the ruling party – and in the end, we are but one of its products. The fact that we despite Copernicus' discovery are still holding on tightly to our anthropocentric perspectives gives shape to our culture – but it does not influence our actual relation to Nature one bit. Our collective fantasies do not have the power to change the laws of Nature.

From the fact that we are incapable of changing the natural world, it logically follows that we have to change our consciousness instead. After all, it is not Nature, but *us* creating this discrepancy. We will have to shift from a linear culture into a more holistic approach: from one-dimensionality to multi-dimensionality, from separation to connectedness, and from specialization to integration.

Instead of plundering our planet, we must relearn how to harvest, how to take care of the Earth, how to live according to the laws of our environment. Taking into account the seasons, the weather, the wind and the complexity of the entire system, we must again become stewards of our planet – completing the Copernican shift.

The life of the human spirit can be understood on three different levels: thinking, feeling and acting. Ever since the seventeenth century, we have been able to *think* that *Homo sapiens* is not the center of the universe, now this knowledge must permeate the two remaining levels: our feelings and our actions. That is why our own personal efforts focus not just on analyzing problems but also (and mostly) on the development of applicable, practical solutions – solutions that honor, respect and even make use of the laws of our natural world. The principle of eternal return, for instance, is a fundamental part of Nature. The sun facilitates the eternal daily, weekly, monthly, seasonal and annual return of the finite: the fruit, the flower, the plant, the tree. What the sun is to the natural world at large, data is to our human-made second Nature: it

facilitates the eternal return of materials and products, in whichever cycle, whenever and wherever in the world. The Turntoo model translates the laws of Nature and applies them to our economic system creating this second Nature. This will enable the preservation of resources by means of new agreements regarding their processing, use and documentation – changing the architecture of the system.

Instead of resisting, and trying to dominate the natural laws, we should bring our actions and interests in agreement with them: riding the rhythmic, cyclical waves of our closed system, instead of letting ever bigger waves wash over us. No longer ignoring the limitations of our planet, but using it's laws to our advantage – like skillful sailors, getting the laws of Nature to push us forward instead of backward.

However, this means change, also inner change, which is not always welcome and comfortable but often even very confronting, as we probably all know from own experience. Yet, the more we resist, the more difficult it becomes. A work of art by Marina Abramovic is a great source of inspiration for us. It shows her at the MoMA in New York in the performance "The Artist is present". During the performance, something unexpected and for the artist even painful happens. The video shows her struggling with the situation. However, as soon as Marina Abramovic decides to accept the situation and literally reaches out to it, the change happens almost by itself, resulting in a powerful transformative experience, also for the audience.

THE HARVEST SOCIETY

The consequences of this new architecture will be immense. Learning to harvest, so that our economy will no longer be dominated by the scarcity of materials and resources, will give us the opportunity to improve billions of lives, by making it far easier for everyone to meet their material needs.

Our economic world and objectives can shift back to their rightful place: that of instruments, instead of a goal in themselves. This, in turn, will create space in our minds for thinking about what we want, as the focus of our lives here on Earth. A society, after all, consists of much more than just an economy. Indeed, there is no such thing as a sealed-off branch of society called 'the economy' or 'the market' – that image is a very recent one. For centuries, economies were regarded as embedded in the whole of social and religious structures. Almost all societies in history were more holistic than the one we live in today: the different parts of society were integrated to a much larger extent than they are now. People were also much more perceptive with regard to the proper relations between their civilization's different parts.

Economics served the community, not just the interests of the individual. It was focused on reciprocity, not just instrumentalism, redistribution, instead of just competition, and collaboration, not just struggle. The function of an economy is to meet the material needs of a people, the function of government and the legal system to (help) shape social relations and norms, and the cultural and spiritual parts of society to fulfill our desire for meaning. The right integration of economics in the whole of society, therefore, is of vital importance: disrupting that balance has many consequences. Today, we are witnessing the dominion of economics over politics, the judiciary and much of the rest of our social and cultural lives, including science, education and the arts.

Our current economy fulfills our daily material needs like food, clothing, housing and transportation – but people have more needs than those: we want to develop ourselves and feel as though we can realize the potential inherent in us. In addition, it is important to us to feel that we are actively participating in shaping the social relations that form the circumstances of our lives. We might even say that humans have three basic needs: self-realization (Freedom), the desire to have some degree of control over the social circumstances of our lives (Equality) and the need for our societies to provide us with a material basis for our existence (Fraternity). In his last work before his death, *Palazzo Regale*, the German artist Joseph Beuys managed to express this principle brilliantly.

The work consists of a space containing seven mirrors and two glass cases, in which a shepherd and a king are respectively displayed. Walking through the installation, visitors see themselves reflected in the mirrors in continuously changing perspectives. For us the artwork represents the two ancient ideas about our role on Earth. The king represents the self-determining sovereignty of humans, the shepherd stands for the modesty and responsibility humans ought to experience with regard to their environment and Nature.[7]

Our new economic model seeks to meet *all* human needs; once we are delivered from the limiting dominance of linear thinking and the struggle for scarce resources and materials, the road to a more egalitarian society will be open. When we stop identifying with what we *have*, we will be free to focus our attention on who we *are*: spiritual beings on a human journey – guests on this Earth.

NOTES

1 Sample, I. (2019). *Earthrise: How the iconic image changed the world*. Retrieved 15 October 2019, from https://www.theguardian.com/science/2018/dec/24/earthrise-how-the-iconic-image-changed-the-world

2 "EPA History." EPA, Environmental Protection Agency. https://www.epa.gov/history

3 Copernicus, N., & Dobrzycki, J. (1978). *On the revolutions*. Baltimore, MD: Johns Hopkins University Press.

4 Galilei, G., & Drake, S. (1953). *Dialogue concerning the two chief world systems, Ptolemaic & Copernican*. Berkeley and Los Angeles: University of California Press

5 Kierkegaard, S., Hong, H. V., Hong, E. H., & Malantschuk, G. (1967). *Søren Kierkegaard's journals and papers*. Bloomington: Indiana University Press.

6 Descartes, R. (1637). *Discours de la methode pour bien conduire sa raison, & chercher la verité dans les sciences*. Retrieved from the Library of Congress. https://www.loc.gov/item/32034972/

7 Joseph Beuys – Palazzo Regale. (1986). https://www.youtube.com/watch?v=BvbV31Oj1Yg. Extract from the film: Joseph Beuys (BBC Arena, 1987).

The Universal Declaration of Human Rights

PREAMBLE A

Whereas recognition of the inherent dignity and of the equal and inalienable rights of all members of the human family is the foundation of freedom, justice and peace in the world,

Whereas it is essential to recognize materials as being both the foundation and an integral part of the fabric of life.

PREAMBLE B

Whereas disregard and contempt for human rights have resulted in barbarous acts, which have outraged the conscience of mankind, and the advent of a world in which human beings shall enjoy freedom of speech and belief and freedom from fear and want has been proclaimed as the highest aspiration of the common people.

Whereas disregard and contempt for material rights have resulted in barbarous acts which have outraged the conscience of mankind, and the advent of a world in which original natural materials shall remain permanently available to perpetuate life as the highest aspiration of life itself.

PREAMBLE C

Whereas it is essential, if man is not to be compelled to have recourse, as a last resort, to rebellion against tyranny and oppression, that human rights should be protected by the rule of law.

Whereas it is essential, if man is not to be compelled to have recourse, as a last resort to rebellion against the effects of human short-sightedness and wasteful behavior, that the rights of materials should be protected by the rule of law.

PREAMBLE D

Whereas it is essential to promote the development of friendly relations between nations.

Whereas it is essential to promote the awareness of the role of materials and the development of a long-term vision on our relation to materials.

PREAMBLE E

Whereas the peoples of the United Nations have in the Charter reaffirmed their faith in fundamental human rights, in the dignity and worth of the human person and in the equal rights of men and women and have determined to promote social progress and better standards of life in larger freedom.

Whereas the peoples of the United Nations have in the Charter reaffirmed their faith in fundamental human rights, in the dignity and worth of the human person and in the equal rights of men and women and have determined to promote social progress and better standards of life in larger freedom, where these -so far- are failing to guard the proper application of materials.

PREAMBLE F

Whereas Member States have pledged themselves to achieve, in co-operation with the United Nations, the promotion of universal respect for and observance of human rights and fundamental freedoms.

Whereas Member States have pledged themselves to achieve, in co-operation with the United Nations, the promotion of universal respect for and observance of human and material rights and fundamental freedoms.

PREAMBLE G

Whereas a common understanding of these rights and freedoms is of the greatest importance for the full realization of this pledge.

Whereas a common understanding of these rights and freedoms is of the greatest importance for the full realization of this pledge.

PREAMBLE H

Now, Therefore THE GENERAL ASSEMBLY proclaims THIS UNI-VERSAL DECLARATION OF HUMAN RIGHTS as a common standard of achievement for all peoples and all nations, to the end that every individual and every organ of society, keeping this Declaration constantly in mind, shall strive by teaching and education to promote respect for these rights and freedoms and by progressive measures, national and international, to secure their universal and effective recognition and observance, both among the peoples of Member States themselves and among the peoples of territories under their jurisdiction.

Now, Therefore THE GENERAL ASSEMBLY proclaims THIS UNI-VERSAL DECLARATION OF MATERIAL RIGHTS as a common standard of achievement for all peoples and all nations, to the end that every individual and every organ of society, keeping this Declaration constantly in mind, shall strive by teaching and education to promote respect for these rights and freedoms and by progressive measures, national and international, to secure their universal and effective recognition and observance, both among the peoples of Member States themselves and among the peoples of territories under their jurisdiction.

ARTICLE 1

All human beings are born free and equal in dignity and rights. They are endowed with reason and conscience and should act towards one another in a spirit of brotherhood.

Materials are the foundation of the fabric of life and form an integral part of it. They are endowed with meaning, purpose and utility and should be treated in a spirit that extends life itself.

ARTICLE 2

Everyone is entitled to all the rights and freedoms set forth in this Declaration, without distinction of any kind, such as race, color, sex, language, religion, political or other opinion, national or social origin, property, birth or other status. Furthermore, no distinction shall be made on the basis of the political, jurisdictional or international status of the country or territory to which a person belongs, whether it be independent, trust, non-self-governing or under any other limitation of sovereignty.

Every material is entitled to all the rights and freedoms set forth in this Declaration, without distinction of any kind, such as composition, phase, color, texture, physical or chemical properties, virgin or manufactured origin, application, value or other status. Further- more, no distinction shall be made on the basis of the political, jurisdictional or international status of the country or territory where a material is situated, whether it be independent, trust, non-self-governing or under any other limitation of sovereignty.

ARTICLE 3

Everyone has the right to life, liberty and security of person.

Every material has the right to contribute to life, to freedom of application and protection of purity.

ARTICLE 4

No one shall be held in slavery or servitude; slavery and the slave trade shall be prohibited in all their forms.

No material shall be mixed in ways where recovery into its original form is impossible; this type of mixing shall be prohibited in all its forms.

ARTICLE 5

No one shall be subjected to torture or to cruel, inhuman or degrading treatment or punishment.

No material shall be subjected to treatment that degrades its future ability to contribute to life.

ARTICLE 6

Everyone has the right to recognition everywhere as a person before the law.

Every material has the right to recognition before the law, just like this has been provided for persons, (business) entities and countries.

ARTICLE 7

All are equal before the law and are entitled without any discrimination to equal protection of the law. All are entitled to equal protection against any discrimination in violation of this Declaration and against any incitement to such discrimination.

All materials are entitled to equal protection against any discrimination in violation of this Declaration and against any incitement to such discrimination.

ARTICLE 8

Everyone has the right to an effective remedy by the competent national tribunals for acts violating the fundamental rights granted him by the constitution or by law.

Every material has the right to be protected by competent national tribunals for acts violating the fundamental rights it has been granted by the constitution of law.

ARTICLE 9

No one shall be subjected to arbitrary arrest, detention or exile.

No material shall be subjected to a state of waste, defined as a state without any associated information or a state of irrecoverability.

ARTICLE 10

Everyone is entitled in full equality to a fair and public hearing by an independent and impartial tribunal, in the determination of his rights and obligations and of any criminal charge against him.

Every material is entitled in full equality to a fair and public assessment by an independent and impartial institution, in the determination of its next destination and application or use when faced with obsolescence in its current form, application or use.

ARTICLE 11-1

(1) Everyone charged with a penal offence has the right to be presumed innocent until proved guilty according to law in a public trial at which he has had all the guarantees necessary for his defense.

(1) Every material faced with a state of loss or waste due to irreversible mixing or loss of data has the right to appropriate research in order to be recovered or updated, until proven pure again.

ARTICLE 11-2

(2) No one shall be held guilty of any penal offence on account of any act or omission, which did not constitute a penal offence, under national or

international law, at the time when it was committed. Nor shall a heavier penalty be imposed than the one that was applicable at the time the penal offence was committed.

(2) No permanent state of irreversibility will ever be accepted on any material, irrespective of the moment the irreversible damage was imposed on the material. The search for recoverability may however be replaced with the search for alternative applications, whichever more life oriented.

ARTICLE 12

No one shall be subjected to arbitrary interference with his privacy, family, home or correspondence, nor to attacks upon his honor and reputation. Everyone has the right to the protection of the law against such interference or attacks.

The data surrounding materials shall not be subjected to arbitrary interference nor to attacks to the systems hosting it. Every material has the right to protection against attacks on its data that prevent it from being considered waste.

ARTICLE 13-1

(1) Everyone has the right to freedom of movement and residence within the borders of each state.

(1) Every material has the right of freedom of movement and application within the borders of each state.

ARTICLE 13-2

(2) Everyone has the right to leave any country, including his own, and to return to his country.

(2) Every material has the right to leave any country, including its country of origin and to return to a state of stock.

ARTICLE 14-1

(1) Everyone has the right to seek and to enjoy in other countries asylum from persecution.

(1) Every material has the right to seek and enjoy in other countries asylum from becoming waste.

ARTICLE 14-2

(2) This right may not be invoked in the case of prosecutions genuinely arising from non-political crimes or from acts contrary to the purposes and principles of the United Nations.

(2) This right may not be used as a justification for economically beneficial dumping of waste in other countries.

ARTICLE 15-1

(1) Everyone has the right to a nationality.

(1) Every unique aggregation of material has the right to a unique identity.

ARTICLE 15-2

(2) No one shall be arbitrarily deprived of his nationality nor denied the right to change his nationality.

(2) No unique aggregation of material shall be arbitrarily deprived of its unique identity.

ARTICLE 16-1

(1) Men and women of full age, without any limitation due to race, nationality or religion, have the right to marry and to found a family. They are entitled to equal rights as to marriage, during marriage and at its dissolution.

(1) Individual original materials of known identity have the right to be merged into a new material provided a trackback remains possible to its history up to that point, along with information on how to undo the merge.

ARTICLE 16-2

(2) Marriage shall be entered into only with the free and full con- sent of the intending spouses.

(2) Merging shall be entered into only if all effects of the resulting material are known, documented and linked to both the new and the old materials.

ARTICLE 16-3

(3) The family is the natural and fundamental group unit of society and is entitled to protection by society and the State.

(3) Materials are the natural and fundamental building blocks of life and are entitled to protection by society and the State.

ARTICLE 17-1

(1) Everyone has the right to own property alone as well as in association with others.

(1) Every material has the right to a guardian that is sincerely concerned with its condition.

ARTICLE 17-2

(2) No one shall be arbitrarily deprived of his property.

(2) No material shall be arbitrarily deprived of its guardian.

ARTICLE 18

Everyone has the right to freedom of thought, conscience and religion; this right includes freedom to change his religion or belief, and freedom, either alone or in community with others and in public or private, to manifest his religion or belief in teaching, practice, worship and observance.

The concept of impermanence is to be considered key to any and all products, appliances, applications, components, etc. as long as they are built from materials. The only thing to be considered permanent, however evolving dynamically, is the concise and collective data covering all materials, their history, current and future applications, everywhere and at any given time.

ARTICLE 19

Everyone has the right to freedom of opinion and expression; this right includes freedom to hold opinions without interference and to seek, receive and impart information and ideas through any media and regardless of frontiers.

Every material has the right to freedom of next application; this right includes freedom to be considered for next application without interference and for the guardian to seek, receive and impart information and ideas through any media and regardless of frontiers.

ARTICLE 20-1

(1) Everyone has the right to freedom of peaceful assembly and association.

(1) Every material has the right to life-supporting aggregation and distribution.

ARTICLE 20-2

(2) No one may be compelled to belong to an association.

(2) No original natural material may be mined as long as stock is available elsewhere

ARTICLE 21

(1) Everyone has the right to take part in the government of his country, directly or through freely chosen representatives.

(2) Everyone has the right of equal access to public service in his country.

(3) The will of the people shall be the basis of the authority of government; this will shall be expressed in periodic and genuine elections,

which shall be by universal and equal suffrage and shall be held by secret vote or by equivalent free voting procedures.

(1) Every material has the right to administration. (2) Every material has the right to equal access to administrative functions and systems worldwide. (3) The will of the people of the mining location shall be the basis of the authority over mined materials; this will be expressed in periodic and genuine elections which shall be by universal and equal suffrage and shall be held by secret vote or by equivalent free voting procedures.

ARTICLE 22

Everyone, as a member of society, has the right to social security and is entitled to realization, through national effort and international co-operation and in accordance with the organization and resources of each State, of the economic, social and cultural rights indispensable for his dignity and the free development of his personality.

Every material, as part of the closed system Earth, has the right to be applied according to the basic design rule for any closed sys-tem, being 'in a closed system all things are equally important to maintain a stable balance'.

ARTICLE 23-1

(1) Everyone has the right to work, to free choice of employment, to just and favorable conditions of work and to protection against unemployment.

(1) Every material has the right to be applied, to free assignment of application, to life supporting conditions and to protection against obsolescence.

ARTICLE 23-2

(2) Everyone, without any discrimination, has the right to equal pay for equal work.

(2) For any material, without any discrimination equal fees shall be charged for equal use in equal applications.

ARTICLE 23-3

(3) Everyone who works has the right to just and favourable remuneration ensuring for himself and his family an existence worthy of human dignity, and supplemented, if necessary, by other means of social protection.

(3) Every material that is applied has the right to a just and favourable cost structure ensuring the extension of life, and to be supplemented, if necessary by additional cost elements for known externalities.

ARTICLE 23-4

(4) Everyone has the right to form and to join trade unions for the protection of his interests.

(4) Every material has the right to be part of trade unions for the protection of materials in their support of life.

ARTICLE 24

Everyone has the right to rest and leisure, including reasonable limitation of working hours and periodic holidays with pay.

Every material has the right to become stock (defined as a semi-permanent state of non-use with the specific objective of preventing anonymity).

ARTICLE 25-1

(1) Everyone has the right to a standard of living adequate for the health and well-being of himself and of his family, including food, clothing, housing and medical care and necessary social services, and the right to security in the event of unemployment, sickness, disability, widowhood, old age or other lack of livelihood in circumstances beyond his control.

(1) Every material has the right to a cost or fee structure that sup- ports its future life as well as its current life, including academic research into data structure and storage, applications, effects, side-effects and externalities.

ARTICLE 25-2

(2) Motherhood and childhood are entitled to special care and assistance. All children, whether born in or out of wedlock, shall enjoy the same social protection.

(2) Virgin and new man-made materials are entitled to special care and attention. Preferably, the installed base of man-made materials shall be retrofitted to the same level of care and attention.

ARTICLE 26-1

(1) Everyone has the right to education. Education shall be free, at least in the elementary and fundamental stages. Elementary education shall be compulsory. Technical and professional education shall be made generally

available and higher education shall be equally accessible to all on the basis of merit.

(1) Every material has the right to academic research and to the communication about known results. Research into effects, side effects and externalities shall be compulsory. Technical results shall be made generally available and advanced research shall be accessible to all on the basis of merit for life.

ARTICLE 26-2

(2) Education shall be directed to the full development of the human personality and to the strengthening of respect for human rights and fundamental freedoms. It shall promote understanding, tolerance and friendship among all nations, racial or religious groups, and shall further the activities of the United Nations for the maintenance of peace.

(2) Academic research shall be directed to the full development of life and to the strengthening of respect for life and the materials that enable it. It shall promote awareness of the importance of the perpetuation of life.

ARTICLE 26-3

(3) Parents have a prior right to choose the kind of education that shall be given to their children.

(3) The people of the original location of an unmined material shall have a prior right to choose the kind of research and potential (non)application of their material.

ARTICLE 27-1

(1) Everyone has the right freely to participate in the cultural life of the community, to enjoy the arts and to share in scientific advancement and its benefits.

(1) Every material has the right to the benefit of scientific advancement, in particular in so far as it allows the material to be reverted into its original state.

ARTICLE 27-2

(2) Everyone has the right to the protection of the moral and material interests resulting from any scientific, literary or artistic production of which he is the author.

(2) Every material has the right to remain part of a larger aggregation that creates value on a new level (e.g. a component or a product).

ARTICLE 28

Everyone is entitled to a social and international order in which the rights and freedoms set forth in this Declaration can be fully realized.

Every material is entitled to a social and international order in which the rights and freedoms set forth in this Declaration can be fully realized.

ARTICLE 29

(1) Everyone has duties to the community in which alone the free and full development of his personality is possible.

(2) In the exercise of his rights and freedoms, everyone shall be subject only to such limitations as are determined by law solely for the purpose of securing due recognition and respect for the rights and freedoms of others and of meeting the just requirements of morality, public order and the general welfare in a democratic society.

(3) These rights and freedoms may in no case be exercised contrary to the purposes and principles of the United Nations.

(1) Transposition to be determined.

(2) Transposition to be determined.

(3) These rights and freedoms may in no case be exercised contrary to the purposes and principles of the United Nations.

ARTICLE 30

Nothing in this Declaration may be interpreted as implying for any State, group or person any right to engage in any activity or to perform any act aimed at the destruction of any of the rights and freedoms set forth herein.

Nothing in this Declaration may be interpreted as implying for any State, group or person any right to engage in any activity or to perform any act aimed at the destruction of any of the rights and freedoms set forth herein.

APPENDIX TWO

Acknowledgments

It is very encouraging to see that ideas for a fundamental transformation of our economic system are gaining growing recognition in our societies, an increasing number of governments, public and private initiatives are addressing this issue these days. However, this great movement also knows champions who have been advocating such a transformation for decades and we feel very privileged that we had the opportunity to meet many of them in person on our journey and are full of gratitude and admiration for their work. This book does not claim to give the sole and comprehensive answer to the challenges we are facing as humanity; rather, it is an attempt to bring our own insights into this important discourse, insights, which we gained from many years of experience in this field.

This book is the result of a long journey that gained an extra momentum with the creation of Turntoo 2010. During this fascinating journey, we have been supported by many people, to whom we would like to express our deep gratitude.

First and most importantly, we want to thank our children for the many hours they have been waiting for us with more or less patience, while we were working on this book, and for being a constant source of inspiration and motivation for our work.

We especially want to thank our former colleague Debby Appleton, our travel companion for many years. With her enthusiasm, dedication and keen spirit, she made an invaluable contribution to the team and our joint work. Together with her and other colleagues, we have developed the ideas, models and concrete examples that are the basis of this book. Marijn Emanuel accompanied us on our personal entrepreneurial journey for over 25 years, with his calm and collected manner, he is an indispensable pillar of support in hectic times. Pablo van den Bosch and Martijn Oostenrijk have given us a wide range of professional support in the recent years; therefore, we are especially grateful that they joined us in our mission as co-founders and directors of Madaster. We are grateful for our collaboration and particularly appreciate their entrepreneurial spirit. We thank Carla Lambij and José Willemsen for their organizational talent and their energy in supporting the team and the book.

Very important for the creation of the book was Roos van Hennekeler. She helped us to translate our concept and ideas for this book into a text, which is accessible and joyful to read, never losing her thrive despite the many rounds of refining and finetuning each chapter went through. Furthermore, she took on the translation of the English version of the book and supported us to develop it further from a Dutch into an international edition.

We owe a great thank you to Walter Stahel, John Elkington and Ken Webster, all three of them long-standing thought leaders in the field of suitability and circular economy who were so kind to read the book and provide us with valuable feedback.

Without the Dutch original edition, this book would not exist. Therefore, we want to thank our Dutch publisher Bertram and De Leeuw for their faith and drive in making the original edition possible. We also want to thank René Warmerdam from the Speakers Academy, who gave the first impulse for the book and connected us to Bertram and De Leeuw. We thank Frank Wiering and William de Bruin for the opportunity to present our ideas in VPRO Tegenlicht. This documentary was the basis for this book.

A special thanks to Jürgen Diessl of Econ, our German publisher for his enthusiasm for our book and the verve with which he drove the project forward. Claudia Cornelsen, the editor of the German edition, was a wonderful editor, with her clear, sharp mind, well-founded questions and suggestions she helped us take the book to a new level. We also want to thank Dave Schmalz for his thorough editing of the English translation of the book and his enthusiastic and encouraging comments. We deeply regret that he passed away before we could share the final result with him.

We are very grateful to Ambassador René van Hell and the Embassy of the Kingdom of the Netherlands in Hungary for making a special first English edition of Material Matters possible. A special thanks to Eva Szabo and Andreou Efsthatios, who helped us to realize this project. Pim van Tol of Monday 9:15 was instrumental in finding the publisher for the English edition of the book and we want to thank him for his professional support as our literacy agent. Thank you also to the Routledge team for their drive and professionalism in publishing the English edition of the book. A great thanks also to the team of Scholz & Friends who designed the beautiful cover for Material Matters. We would also like to mention Hans Rietveld of OneDesign, who developed the name and the logo of Turntoo for us.

Our thanks also go to our colleagues who are or have been involved in our work in Turntoo over the recent years: Eric de Ruijter, Rachel Louiws, Murkje Kingma, Richard Greil, Rob Oomen, Bas Berck, Ruben van Doorn, Ronald de Graan, Dennis Groteboer, Douwe Jan Joustra, Ariane Kaper, Peter Klaassen, Erik Mulder, Kaan Ozdurak, Henk Rebel, Mirjam Schmull and Esmé Stevens.

People who have supported us with their talent and professionalism: Saskia Baan, Koos van den Berg, Walter Link, Matthijs Schouten and Sander de Wolf. There were also many people who helped us, especially in the initial phase, when our ideas were still completely new and the Term Circular Economy was still completely unknown: Peter Blom, Rick Boomer, Serena Borghero, Michael Braungart, Sharona Ceha, John Elkington, Wouter Van Dieren, Stef Kranendijk, Willem Lageweg, Ellen MacArthur, the Ellen MacArthur Foundation, Marjan Minnesma, Robert Metzke, Pablo Smolders, Herman Wijffels and Catharena Countess von Bernstorff.

A decisive element for the development of our ideas was and is their actualization in concrete projects. They could only emerge in collaboration with others. We thank the people with whom we were able to realize the first projects at a time when being involved in circularity was still a novelty: Debby Beitsma, Bart Blokland, Henk Bol, Henk de Bruin, Mellouki Cadat, Onno Dwars, Eric Heutinck, Frans van Houten, Rob Kragt, Markus Laubscher, Sabien van der Leij, John Nederstigt, Cecile van Oppen, Frank Snijders, Arthur Thomaes, Erik Toenhake, Alex Tuinstra, Marc Unger, Wim op het Veld, Dirk van der Ven, Frank van der Vloed, Helene van der Vloed, Magdalena Völker and Dorien van der Weele.

As our ideas evolved over the course of the years also our activities did. Therefore, we would like to thank Pablo van den Bosch and Martijn Oostenrijk Marijn Emanuel, Jeroen Vermeulen and Ronald Eleveld with whom we founded Madaster in 2017. A great thank you to the team who is building Madaster in the Netherlands and abroad Sander Beeks, Michiel Lankamp, Stéphanie Guyot, Jeroen Broersma, Richard Greil, Germien Cox, Sander Hoek, Marloes Fischer, Patrick Bergmann, Claudius Frank, Leif I. Nordhus, Anstein Skinnarland, Johan Klaps, Vincent Verbruggen, Ida Mae de Waal. Joanca van den Bosch, Erik Bronsvoort, Rob Oomen, Sander Bosman, and Erik van Esch also supported us for a while. And a special thank you to Marzia Traverso, Ken Webster and Carol Lemmens, who joined the initiative as board members of the Madaster Foundation.

We would also like to thank the companies who support the development of Madaster as 'Kennedy's' in terms of content and finances, a network which is continuously growing internationally. Abn Amro, Accumulatata Real Estate, Akd, Alliander, Allianz Real Estate, Arcade, Architecten cie, Art Invest, Arup, Assar architecten, Aspelin Ramm Eiendom, Assiduus Developement, ATP architekten ingenieure, Ballast Nedam, Baukom Group, Becken Holding, Beddeleem, Berlin Hyp, BDO, BDG Business Development, Ninst Architects, Bouwend Nederland, Bureau Boot, Cad & company, caspar.architects, City of Antwerp, Commerz Real AG, Conix RDMB, Cordeel, Cores Developments, COWI, Deerns, Drees & Sommer, Dutch Green Building Council, Dura Vermeer, Eberhard Bau, Earth and Eternity, ENA Experts, Entra, Epea, Heijmans, Henning Larsen Architects, Ghelamco, Grohe, GSJ Advocaten, Holcim, Imd Raadgevende Ingenieurs, Immobel, Ing Real Estate Finance, Interalu, Interboden, Jan de Nul Group, Kaldewei, KPMG, Konder Wessels, Kubus, Lidner Group, List Bau, Losinger Marazzi, Mitsubishi Elevator Europe, Mortelmans van Tricht, Nemetschek, Nextensa, Nij Smellinghe, OVG Real Estate / EDGE Technology, ProRail, PwC, Rabobank, Rambøll, Ratio Arkitetker, Redevco Foundation, Ripkens Wiesenkämper, Schiphol Group, Schiphol Asset Management, Schüco International AG, Smedwig Eiendom, Swiss Railways SBB, Swiss Prime Site, Swiss Re, Statsbygg, Sotrebrand Eiendom, Sweco, Tbi, Triocare, Triodos Bank, Value One, Veni, VolkerWessels, Vonovia / BUWOG, Vorm bouw, WhiteWood, Yugening.

We thank Professor Jan Peter Balkenende, former prime minister of the Netherlands and now chairman of the Major Alliance and his team in 2018 Guus Kramer, Lotte Holvast and Marie-Claire Troost, for their support in promoting the Universal Declaration of Material Rights. We thank the Carnegie Foundation for the opportunity to discuss the Universal Declaration of Material Rights for the first time at an international conference with high-level representatives at the Peace Palace in The Hague, during the Carnegie Peace Conversations in September 2018. We also would like to thank Sandra Pellegrom then member of the Permanent Mission of the Kingdom of the Netherlands to the United Nations in New York, who helped us to present the Universal Declaration of Material Rights to delegates of the United Nations on December 10, 2018.

We are very grateful to the DOEN Foundation, and especially to Jeffrey Prins and Steve Elbers. They made Turntoo possible with their financial support during the start-up phase.

We would like to thank Magdalene Rau, Karl Fleschenberg and Mr. D. Müller for their information about the Hauberg.

Without teachers and mentors, we would never have gone this route, so we would like to express our gratitude to Peter Ferger, Otto-Paul Hessel, Paulgerd Jesberg †, Matthias Krups and Joseph Wies.

We do not want to forget the people from our personal environment who have allowed us to work on our ideas for this book: Sybelle, Willie and Martin, Tanja and Aino. We also want to thank our parents, Magdalene, Ulrich †, Stefanie and Wilhelm who gave us the foundations of our lives and taught us to pursue the paths our hearts believe in.

Sources

INTRODUCTION

1. Boulding, K. (1973). Anyone who believes in indefinite growth in anything physical, on a physically finite planet, is either mad or an economist. Statement made at: U.S. Congress, Energy Reorganization Act of 1973: Hearings, Ninety-third Congress, First Session, on H.R. 11510, U.S. Government Printing Office, p. 248. https://www.govinfo.gov/app/details/CHRG-93hhrg25108O

2. Rockström, J., Steffen, W., Noone, K., et al. (2009). "A safe operating space for humanity." *Nature*, Vol. 461, pp. 472–475. https://doi.org/10.1038/461472a; "The Nine Planetary Boundaries." *The Nine Planetary Boundaries – Stockholm Resilience Centre*. The Stockholm Reslience Institute. https://www.stockholmresilience.org/research/-planetary-boundaries/the-nine-planetary-boundaries.html

CHAPTER 1

1. Kettering, C. (1929). "The key to economic prosperity…" quoted from The End of Work (1995) by Jeremy Rifkin, p. 19.
2. Livermore's Centennial Light Bulb. (2021). https://www. centennialbulb.org
3. Marcuse, H. (1991). *One-dimensional man: Studies in the ideology of advanced industrial society.* Boston, MA: Beacon Press.
4. Krajewski, M. (2014). *The great lightbulb conspiracy.* IEEE Spectrum. https://spectrum.ieee. org/tech-history/dawn-of-electronics/the-great-lightbulb-conspiracy
5. Dannoritzer, C. (2010). *The light bulb conspiracy.* https:// topdocumentaryfilms.com/light-bulb-conspiracy/
6. Kreiß, C. (2001). *Geplanter Verschleiß: Wie die Industrie uns zu immer mehr und immer schnellerem Konsum antreibt – und wie wir uns dagegen wehren können.* Berlin: Europaverlag.
7. Pynchon, T. (1973). *Gravity's rainbow.* New York: Viking Press.
8. London, B. (1932). *Ending the depression through planned obsolescence.* https://www.semanticscholar.org/paper/Ending-the-Depression-through-Planned-Obsolescence-London/622892147cfe3 c4567d0d92d528394423d93e5a4
9. Glenn A. (2003). *Industrial strength design: How Brooks Stevens shaped your world.* Cambridge, MA: MIT Press.
10. Appliance Spare Parts Availability and the Law. (2012, updated 2016). https://www.ukwhitegoods.co.uk/help/spare-parts/general-spare-part-help/3473-appliance-spare-parts-and-the-law
11. Brönneke, T., & Wechsler, A. (2015). *Obsoleszenz interdisziplinär,* Schriftenreihe des Instituts für Europäisches Wirtschafts-und Verbraucheerrecht e.V. Band 37, Baden-Baden.
12. Connexion (2018). 'Built-in obsolescence' study targets women's tights. Retrieved from https://www.connexionfrance.com/French-news/Built-in-obsolescence-study-targets-women-s-tights
13. They Time Those Things, designforlongevity.com. https:// designforlongevity.com/videos/they-time-those-things

14. Eco@Work (2016). *Obsolescence, causes, effects, strategies.* Oeko Institut Germany. https://www.oeko.de/fileadmin/magazin/2016/02/ecoatwork_02_2016_en.pdf

15. European Environment Agency (2020). *Europe's consumption in a circular economy: The benefits of longer-lasting electronics.* https://www.eea.europa.eu/publications/europe2019s-consumption-in-a-circular/benefits-of-longer-lasting-electronics

16. Roser, M. (2019). *Working hours.* OurWorldInData.org. https://ourworldindata.org/working-hours

17. Ip, G. (2016). *The economy's hidden problem: We're out of big ideas.* https://www.wsj.com/articles/the-economys-hidden-problem-were-out-of-big-ideas-1481042066

18. Sloan, A. P. (1972). *My years with general motors.* Garden City, NY: Doubleday.

19. Prakash, S., Schleicher, T., Dehoust, G., Gsell, M., & Stamminger, R. (2016). *Einfluss der Nutzungsdauer von Produkten auf ihre Umweltwirkung: Schaffung einer Informationsgrundlage und Entwicklung von Strategien gegen "Obsoleszenz".* Study by Ökoinstitut commission by the German Umweltbundesamt, Retrieved from: https://www.umweltbundesamt.de/sites/default/files/medien/378/publikation/texte_11_2016_einfluss_der_nutzungsdauer_von_produkten_obsoleszenz.pdf

20. Simon Kucher & Partners (2019). *Relevance and future users of Apple TV+.* https://www.simon-kucher.com/nl/about/media-center/new-study-streaming-services-rapidly-replacing-traditional-tv

21. Gartner (2017). Market Share: PCs, Ultramobiles and Mobile Phones, All Countries, 4Q17.

22. Gartner Press Release (2021). 'Gartner Says Worldwide Smartphone Sales to Grow 11% by 2021. https://www.gartner.com/en/newsroom/-press-releases/2021-02-03-gartner-says-worldwide-smartphone-sales-to-grow-11-percent-in-2021

23. U.S. Geological Survey (2006). *Recycled cell phones – A treasure trove of valuable metals.* Fact Sheet 2006-3097, Department of Interior, July. https://pubs.usgs.gov/fs/2006/3097/fs2006-3097.pdf

24. Electronics Take Back Coalition (2014). *Facts and figures on e-waste and recycling*, http://www.electronicstakeback.com/wp-content/uploads/Facts_and_Figures_on_EWaste_and_Recycling.pdf

25. Curtis, A. (2002). *The century of the self*. BBC documentary series.

26. Remy, N., Speelman, E., & Swartz, S. (2016). *Style that's sustainable: A new fast-fashion formula*. McKinsey. https://www.mckinsey.com/business-functions/sustainability/our-insights/style-thats-sustainable-a-new-fast-fashion-formula

27. EllenMacArthurFoundation (2017). *A new textiles economy*. https://www.ellenmacarthurfoundation.org/assets/downloads/A-New-Textiles-Economy_Full-Report_Updated_1-12-17.pdf

28. House of Commons Environmental Audit Committee (2019). *Fixing fashion: Clothing consumption and sustainability*. https://publications.parliament.uk/pa/cm201719/cmselect/cmenvaud/1952/1952.pdf

29. Babbitt, C. W., Kahhat, R., Williams, E., & Babbitt, G. A. (2009). "Evolution of product lifespan and implications for environmental assessment and management: A case study of personal computers in higher education." *Environmental Science & Technology*, Vol. 43, No. 13, pp. 5106–5112.

30. Siegle, L. (2013). *What is the lifespan of a laptop?* The Guardian environment https://www.theguardian.com/environment/2013/jan/13/lifespan-laptop-pc-planned-obsolescence

31. Geere, D. (2016). Electronic product lifespans are getting shorter. https://www.wired.co.uk/article/product-lifespans

32. Consumer Reports (2019). *How long will your appliance last?* https://www.consumerreports.org/appliances/how-long-will-your-appliances-last/

33. Han, B.-C. (2017). *Psychopolitics: Neoliberalism and new technologies of power*. London: Verso Books.

34. IRP (2019). *Global resources outlook 2019: Natural resources for the future we want*. Oberle, B., Bringezu, S., Hatfeld-Dodds, S., Hellweg, S., Schandl, H., Clement, J., Cabernard, L., Che, N., Chen, D., Droz-Georget, H., Ekins, P., FischerKowalski, M., Flörke, M., Frank, S., Froemelt, A., Geschke, A., Haupt, M., Havlik, P., Hüfner, R., Lenzen, M., Lieber, M., Liu, B., Lu, Y., Lutter, S., Mehr, J., Miatto, A., Newth,

D., Oberschelp, C., Obersteiner, M., Pfster, S., Piccoli, E., Schaldach, R., Schüngel, J., Sonderegger, T., Sudheshwar, A., Tanikawa, H., van der Voet, E., Walker, C., West, J., Wang, Z., Zhu, B. *A report of the international resource panel.* Nairobi, Kenya: United Nations Environment Programme.

35. Phonebloks: https://phonebloks.com
36. Brandalism: http://brandalism.ch
37. Repaircafé: https://repaircafe.org/en/visit/
38. We Have the Right to Repair Everything We Own, Ifixit: https://www.ifixit.com/Right-to-Repair/Intro
39. *BBC News* (2018). *Apple and Samsung fined by Italian authorities over slow phones.* BBC News, https://www.bbc.com/news/technology-45963943

CHAPTER 2

1. Cook, K. (2014). *Kitty Genovese: The murder, the bystanders, the crime that changed America.* New York: W. W. Norton & Company.
2. *Diffusion of Responsibility. Encyclopædia Britannica,* Encyclopædia Britannica, Inc. https://www.britannica.com/topic/bystander-effect/Diffusion-of-responsibility
3. Philpott, T (2014). *Are your delicious, healthy almonds killing bees?* Mother Jones. https://www.motherjones.com/food/2014/04/california-almond-farms-blamed-honeybee-die/
4. Ecolabel Index. http://www.ecolabelindex.com/
5. Atkinson, L. (2014). *Wild west' of eco-labels: Sustainability claims are confusing consumers.* The Guardian, Guardian News and Media. https://www.theguardian.com/sustainable-business/eco-labels-sustainability-trust-corporate-government
6. Meadows, D. H. [and others]. (1972). *The limits to growth; a report for the Club of Rome's project on the predicament of mankind.* New York: Universe Books.
7. Forti, V., Baldé, C. P., Kuehr, R., & Bel, G. (2020) The Global E-waste Monitor 2020. http://ewastemonitor.info/

8. The Economics of Ecosystems and Biodiversity (TEEB) is a global initiative focused on "making nature's values visible". Its principal objective is to mainstream the values of biodiversity and ecosystem services into decision-making at all levels. https://www.teebweb.org

9. FAO (2017). *The future of food and agriculture – Trends and challenges.* Rome. http://www.fao.org/3/a-i6583e.pdf

10. PriceWaterhouseCooper (2011). *Minerals and metals scarcity in manufacturing: The ticking time bomb.* https://www.pwc.com/ua/en/industry/metal_mining/assets/impact_of_minerals_metals_scarcity_on_business.pdf

11. McCarthy, N. (2014). China Used More Concrete in 3 Years than the U.S. Used in the Entire 20th Century [Infographic]. *Forbes*, Forbes Magazine. https://www.forbes.com/sites/niallmccarthy/2014/12/05/-china-used-more-concrete-in-3-years-than-the-u-s-used-in-the-entire-20th-century-infographic/

12. Prior, T., Giurco, D., Mudd, G., Mason, L., & Behrisch, J. (2012). *Resource depletion peak minerals and the implications for sustainable resource management, Global Environmental Change.* https://www.academia.edu/3632952/Resource_depletion_peak_minerals_and_the_implications_for_sustainable_resource_management

13. Beiser, V. (2017). Sand mining: The global environmental crisis you've never heard of. *The Guardian*, Guardian News and Media. Retrieved from https://www.theguardian.com/cities/2017/feb/27/-sand-mining-global-environmental-crisis-never-heard

14. Forti, V., Baldé, C. P., Kuehr, R., & Bel, G. (2020) *The global E-waste monitor 2020.* http://ewastemonitor.info/

15. MDR, Exact. (2013). *Warum alte Küchengeräte aus dem Osten heute noch funktionieren.* T-Online, Lifestyle: Besser Leben. https://www.t-online.de/leben/id_62366296/warum-alte-elektrogeraete-aus-dem-osten-heute-noch-funktionieren.html

CHAPTER 3

1. Mc Luhann, M. (Winter 1974). "On spaceship earth there are no passengers." Quote from "At the Moment of Sputnik" in *Journal of Communication*.
2. Howell, E., & Hickock, K. (2020). *Apollo 13: The moon-mission that dodged disaster*. Space.com, https://www.space.com/17250-apollo-13-facts.html
3. The Truman Show, 1998, Paramount Pictures.
4. Hofstadter, D. (2007). *I am a strange loop*. New York: Basic Books.
5. Lorenz E. (1972). "Does the flap of a butterfly's wings in Brazil set off a tornado in Texas?" *American Association for the Advancement of Science*.
6. Smith, A. (1723–1790). *The wealth of nations/Adam Smith*; Introduction by Robert Reich; Edited, with Notes, Marginal Summary, and Enlarged Index by Edwin Cannan. New York: Modern Library, 2000.
7. Maslow, A. H. (1943). "A theory of human motivation." *Psychological Review*, Vol. 50, No. 4, pp. 370–396.
8. Marshall, G. (2014). *Understand faulty thinking to tackle climate change*. New Scientist, https://www.newscientist.com/article/-mg22329820-200-understand-faulty-thinking-to-tackle-climate-change/

CHAPTER 4

1. Mark, J. J. (2016). The Step Pyramid of Djoser. *Ancient History Encyclopedia*, Ancient History Encyclopedia. Retrieved from www.ancient.eu/article/862/the-step-pyramid-of-djoser/
2. Forti, V., Baldé, C. P., Kuehr, R., & Bel, G. (2020). *The global E-waste monitor 2020*. http://ewastemonitor.info/

3. Ellen MacArthur Foundation (2015). *Growth within: A circular economy vision for a competitive Europe.* https://www. ellenmacarthurfoundation.org/assets/downloads/publications/ EllenMacArthurFoundation_Growth-Within_July15.pdf

4. Nepley (2008). *Kitchens of the future.* https://www.youtube. com/watch?v=TiACOLuYlJ4&t=185s

5. Asurion (2019). *Americans aren't taking a break from their phones.* https://www.asurion.com/connect/tech-tips/americans-arent-taking-a-break-from-their-phones

6. Page, C. (2014). *There are now more active mobile devices than humans.* The INQUIRER. https://www.theinquirer.net/inquirer/ news/2374525/there-are-now-more-active-mobile-devices-than-humans

7. "Telekom-Vorstand Claudia Nemat Im Interview." (2018). *Teachtoday*, Helliwood Media & Education. https://www.teachtoday. de/Informieren/Digitale_Kommunikation/2575_Claudia_Nemat_ im_Interview.htm

8. Reday-Mulvey, G., Stahel, W. R., & Commission of the European Communities. (1977). *The potential for substituting manpower for energy: Final report 30 July 1977 for the Commission of the European Communities.* Geneva, Switzerland: Battelle, Geneva Research Centre.

9. Earth Overshoot Day, *Footprint Network.* https://www. footprintnetwork.org/our-work/earth-overshoot-day/

10. Members of the Stratigraphy Commission of the Geological Society of London (2008). The Anthropocene Epoch: Today's Context for Governance and Public Policy. The Geological Society, The Geological Society of London. Retrieved from https://www.geolsoc. org.uk/Geoscientist/Letters/2008/The-Anthropocene-Epoch-todays-context-for-governance-and-public-policy

11. World Commission on Environment and Development (1987). *Our common future.* Oxford: Oxford University Press.

12. McDonough, W., & Braungart, M. (2009). *Cradle to cradle: Remaking the way we make things.* London: Vintage.

13. "What Is Biomimicry?" *Biomimicry Institute.* Website: https:// biomimicry.org/what-is-biomimicry/

14. *Wuppertal Institut Für Klima, Umwelt, Energie*. Website: https://wupperinst.org/en

15. Elkington, J. 25 Years ago I coined the phrase 'Triple Bottom Line.' Here's why it's time to rethink it. *Harvard Business Review*, 13 September. 2018. https://hbr.org/2018/06/25-years-ago-i-coined-the-phrase-triple-bottom-line-heres-why-im-giving-up-on-it

16. Ellen MacArthur Foundation (2012). *Towards the circular economy*. Report Volume 1. London: Ellen MacArthur Foundation.

17. Machiavelli, N., & Wootton, D. (1995). *The prince*. Indianapolis, IN: Hackett Pub. Co.

CHAPTER 5

1. Turntoo Website. http://turntoo.com/

2. Schaller, B. (2018). *The new automobility: Lyft, Uber and the Future of American Cities*. Retrieved from https://www.schallerconsult.com/rideservices/automobility.htm

3. "Een Abonnement Op Wassen." *Bluemovement*. https://www.bluemovement.nl/

4. Rogers, E. M. (1962). *Diffusion of innovations*. New York: Free Press of Glencoe.

5. "Circular Denim: A World Without Waste." *Jeans*. https://mudjeans.eu/

6. A world without waste: Covering an icon in denim to be more sustainable. https://about.ikea.com/en/sustainability/a-world-without-waste/covering-an-icon-in-denim-to-be-more-sustainable

7. "Better Than New." *Worn Wear*, Patagonia. https://wornwear.patagonia.com/

CHAPTER 6

1. Carlowitz, H. C. (1713). *Sylvicultura oeconomica: Anweisisungen zur wilden Baumzucht*. Johann Friedrich Braun, Leipzig.

2. Prior, E. (2016). How much gold is there in the world? *BBC News.* https://www.bbc.com/news/magazine-21969100

3. Jaiswal, A., Samuel, C., Patel, B. S., & Kumar, M. (2015). "Go Green with WEEE: Eco-friendly approach for handling E-waste." *Procedia Computer Science*, Vol. 46, 1317–1324.

4. Voakes, G. (2012). *The lesser-known facts about e-waste recycling.* Hack College, Business Insider. https://www.businessinsider. com/the-lesser-known-facts-about-e-waste-recycling-2012-10?international=true&r=US&IR=T

    Bankmycell (2019). *Cell phone recycling & e-waste facts.* rhttps://www.bankmycell.com/support/e-waste-cell-phone-recycling-facts#stats2

5. Palmer, J. (2016). "Parmenides." *Stanford Encyclopedia of Philosophy.* Stanford University. Retrieved from https://plato.stanford. edu/entries/parmenides/

6. Brand, S. (2012). How buildings learn: The oak beams of New College Oxford. Retrieved from https://www.youtube. com/watch?v=YqH4eWR7jDQ

7. Bard, A., & Söderqvist, J. (2012). *The futurica trilogy*. Stockholm: Stockholm Texts.

8. Deming, D. (2010). *Science and technology in world history, Volume 1: "The ancient world and classical civilization."* Jefferson, NC: McFarland & Company.

9. UNEP. Energy efficiency for buildings. Paris. http://www. studiocollantin.eu/pdf/UNEP%20Info%20sheet%20-%20EE%20 Buildings.pdf

10. Aguilar, C. (2015). Alliander HQ/RAU architects. *ArchDaily*, ArchDaily. Retrieved from www.archdaily. com/777783/alliander-hq-rau-architects

11. Astbury, J. (2019). Thatched reeds cover egg-shaped Tij observatory for watching birds. *Dezeen*, Dezeen, 17 June 2019. https://www. dezeen.com/2019/05/11/tij-bird-observatory-rau-architects-scheelhoek-nature-reserve/

12. Tapia, D. (2019). Triodos Bank/RAU architects. *ArchDaily*, ArchDaily. https://www.archdaily.com/926357/triodos-bank-rau-architects

CHAPTER 7

1. Cleppe, P. (2015). The case of the Greek Land Registry. *Open Europe*, Open Europe. https://openeurope.org.uk/today/blog/reforming-greece-easier-said-done-never-ending-case-land-registry/
   Lefteris, P. (2019). End in sight for Greece's long quest to complete National Land Registry. *Reuters*, Thomson Reuters. https://www.reuters.com/article/us-greece-landregistry-idUSKCN1QW23B
   Lialios, G. (2021). Municipalities Ignoring Land Registry. *EKathimerini.com*, ΚΑΘΗΜΕΡΙΝΕΣ ΕΚΔΟΣΕΙΣ ΜΟΝΟΠΡΟΣΩΠΗ Α.Ε. Εθν.Μακαρίου & Φαληρέως. https://www.ekathimerini.com/news/261830/municipalities-ignoring-land-registry/

2. EIA (2015). Stealing the last forest. Environmental Investigation Agency. https://www.illegal-logging.info/sites/files/chlogging/EIA%20(2015)%20Romania%20Report.pdf

3. UNEP. Energy efficiency for buildings. Paris. http://www.studiocollantin.eu/pdf/UNEP%20Info%20sheet%20-%20EE%20Buildings.pdf

4. Ruuska, A., & Häkkinen, T. (2014). Material efficiency of building construction. *Buildings*, Vol. 4(3), pp. 266–294. https://doi.org/10.3390/buildings4030266

5. Romers, G., & Duijvestein, P., et al. (2020). *Circulaire business cases in de MRA*. Bouw en Sloopafval. https://www.metabolic.nl/publications/circulaire-business-cases-mra-bouw-sloopafval/

6. EU Circular Material Use Rate. Eurostat, 12 March 2020. https://ec.europa.eu/eurostat/web/products-eurostat-news/-/ddn-20200312-1

7. Mattauch, C. (2021). Eine Datenbank, die das Bauen revolutionieren könnte, Süddeuttsche Zeitung. https://www.sueddeutsche.de/wirtschaft/bauen-gebaeude-material-datenbank-madaster-1.5404136

8. Mattauch, C. (2021). Eine Datenbank, die das Bauen revolutionieren könnte, Süddeuttsche Zeitung. https://www.sueddeutsche.de/wirtschaft/bauen-gebaeude-material-datenbank-madaster-1.5404136

9. Madaster. https://www.madaster.com/en
   Madaster Foundation. https://madasterfoundation.com/

CHAPTER 8

1. Eleanor Roosevelt: Address to the United Nations General Assembly (1948). http://www.kentlaw.edu/faculty/bbrown/classes/HumanRigh tsSP10/CourseDocs/2EleanorRoosevelt.pdf
2. Sitra (2018). *The circular economy – A powerful force for climate mitigation, Transformative innovation for prosperous and low-carbon industry*. Stockholm: Material Economics Sverige AB. https://www. sitra.fi/en/publications/circular-economy-powerful-force-climate-mitigation/
3. Hieminga, G. (2017). *Circular solutions to water shortage*. ING Economics Department. https://www.ing.nl/media/ING_EBZ_ circular-solutions-to-water-shortage_tcm162-121757.pdf
4. Fricsa, S., Huggins, C., & Unruh, J. (2012). *Land and conflict*. New York: United Nations Interagency Framework Team for Preventive Action. https://www.un.org/en/land-natural-resources-conflict/pdfs/ EU-UN%20Introduction%20and%20overview.pdf
5. "About the Sustainable Development Goals – United Nations Sustainable Development." United Nations, United Nations. www. un.org/sustainabledevelopment/sustainable-development-goals/

CHAPTER 9

1. Achterhuis, H. (2010) *De utopie van de vrije markt*. Rotterdam: Lemniscaat.
2. Hardin, G. (1968). "The tragedy of the commons." *Science*, Vol. 162, pp. 1243–1248.
3. Ostrom, E. (2015). *Governing the commons: The evolution of institutions for collective action* (Canto Classics). Cambridge: Cambridge University Press. doi:10.1017/CBO9781316423936
4. Alaska Permanent Fund Corporation. https://apfc.org/

CHAPTER 10

1. Sample, I. (2019). *Earthrise: How the iconic image changed the world.* Retrieved 15 October 2019, from https://www.theguardian.com/science/2018/dec/24/earthrise-how-the-iconic-image-changed-the-world

2. "EPA History." EPA, Environmental Protection Agency. https://www.epa.gov/history

3. Copernicus, N., & Dobrzycki, J. (1978). *On the revolutions.* Baltimore, MD: Johns Hopkins University Press.

4. Galilei, G., & Drake, S. (1953). *Dialogue concerning the two chief world systems, Ptolemaic & Copernican.* Berkeley and Los Angeles, University of California Press

5. Kierkegaard, S., Hong, H. V., Hong, E. H., & Malantschuk, G. (1967). *Søren Kierkegaard's journals and papers.* Bloomington: Indiana University Press.

6. Descartes, R. (1637). *Discours de la methode pour bien conduire sa raison, & chercher la verité dans les sciences.* Retrieved from the Library of Congress. https://www.loc.gov/item/32034972/

7. Joseph Beuys – Palazzo Regale. (1986). https://www.youtube.com/watch?v=BvbV31Oj1Yg

Illustrations

Every effort has been made to contact copyright holders for their permission to reprint the image opposite in this book. The publishers would be grateful to hear from any copyright holder who is not here acknowledged and will undertake to rectify any errors or omissions in future editions of this book.

Earthrise, Bill Anders, NASA

Tower of Babel, Abel Grimmer (1570–1620)

Centennial Bulb, Richard Jones

Electronic Waste, PN-Photo, iStock

Wasteful Business Models, Turntoo

Wastepile in Guiy, China, unknown

Wastestream Beirut, Ghazal Amar, Alamy Photo

STS-116 Shuttle Mission, NASA

Apollo 13, NASA

Secrets of the mind, Andrew Rich, iStock

Internal gears of wristwatch, Hernan Caputo

Fairground attraction in Colgne, Ben Pawils

Djoser Pyramid, Jakish, iStock

Part of Roller Coaster, iStock

MUD Jeans detail, MUD Jeans

Lamp, Hans Lebbe

Man with Bosch fridge, Turntoo

Lounge at Schiphol Airport, Turntoo

Finger print, Colorbox

Sylviacultura oeconmica, Thomas Weidner

Bird Observatory, Katja Effting, Design RAU

Liander Headquarter, Marcel van der Burg, Design RAU

Roofconstruction Liander, RAU

Triodos Bank, Alexander van Berge, Design RAU

Bird Observatory, Katja Effting, Design RAU

Online platform Madaster, Sander Bosman

Madaster Logo, Design Hans Rietveld

United Nations Photo, Cia Pak

Mrs. Eleanor Roosevelt holding poster with UDHR, United Nations

Cobalt Mine Congo, Fairphone

Gear wheels in machinery, iStock

Material-as-a-Service, Turntoo-Model, Turntoo

Wood log pattern, rawpixel ID 6165784

Earthrise, Bill Anders, NASA

Revolutionibus orbium coelestium, Copernicus

Marina Abromovic, The Artist Is Present, MoMA NY 2010, Scott Rudd

Joseph Beuys, Palazzo Regale 1985, Esther Hecht

Library Check Out Sheet, Turntoo

8/9/9

0 7 SEP 2004   13/10/09

15-2-11

3 0 NOV 2004   30 6 11   601   29-5-15
                18-9-11

                 2 5 10 11

2 1 DEC. 2004   17-1-12

                 4-1-2

1 8 JAN 2005   21-2-12
8 MRT 2005   6 3 12

3 5.05.   203-12

1 3 SEP 2005   21-4-12

1 8 OKT 2005   12-6-12

- 8 NOV. 2005   11-9-12

                16-10-12

                20 11 12.

1 4 MRT 2006   29-1-13

1 1 APR. 2006   5-3-13

                9 4 13

9 MEI 2006   14-5-13
- 4 SEP 2007   4-6-13

- 4 DEC 2007   12 11 13

22-1-08   3-12-13

16/9/08   7 1 14.

14-10-8   2005 14

16-12-08   20-3-15

                9.4.15
3/3/09   23 4 15

12/5/09

DON'T OWN – ENJOY!

We need to organize the economy as a library

-- Thomas Rau

Do you already know this book?

Material Matters has inspired me and I therefore gladly give it to you for inspiration.

Read by.. Date...............

Read by.. Date...............

Read by.. Date...............

Read by.. Date...............

Read by.. Date...............

Read by.. Date...............

Read by.. Date...............

About the authors

THOMAS RAU

Thomas Rau is an architect, entrepreneur, innovator and recognized thought leader on sustainability and circular economy. His office RAU has been recognized for being at the forefront of producing innovative CO_2 neutral, energy positive and circular buildings as a norm. Thomas was elected as Dutch Architect of the Year 2013 and awarded with the ARC13 Oeuvre Award for his widespread contribution in both promoting and realizing sustainable architecture and bringing awareness of the circular economy through international delivered lectures, TV documentaries, TED talks and publications. In 2016, he was nominated for the Circular Economy leadership Award of the World Economic Forum. In 2021, he received the Circular Hero Award by the Dutch Ministry of Infrastructure.

SABINE OBERHUBER

S abine Rau-Oberhuber is an economist; together with Thomas Rau, she cofounded Turntoo, one of the first companies in the world focusing on the transition to a circular economy. Sabine is a renowned expert on circular economy; together with her team at Turntoo, she assists corporate clients and public institutions in the development and implementation of circular business models and management strategies and facilitates the transition to a circular economy. She studied economics at the Freie Wilhelms University in Münster (Germany) and received her Master of Management from the ESCP (EAP) European School of Management in Paris, Oxford and Berlin.

ACTIVITIES

TURNTOO

Turntoo is known for breakthrough innovations such as the Light-as-a-Service (Circular Lighting) model developed with Philips Lighting, or washing machines on performances basis with Bosch, which have become iconic projects for the circular economy.

Turntoo regards the necessary transformation taking place on four levels: the design of products and supply chains; the financial and business models involved; the data and IT infrastructure supporting the transition and the mental transformation leading to a new way of thinking.

RAU

RAU Architects is seen as a pioneer in circular buildings. RAU designed the first circular building as a raw materials depot in the municipality of Brummen in 2013 and the first circular net energy positive building for network provider Liander in 2015. The recently finished headquarters of Triodos Bank is the first fully circular, re-constructible office building made of wood.

MADASTER

Madaster Rau and Oberhuber initiated Madaster, a central registry
for material, the cadaster for materials. Madaster is an open online
platform for material passports founded in 2017. Madaster's is rolled out
internationally and is currently operational in 8 European countries. For
its potential for systemic change, Madaster won the Digital Top 50 Award
for Social Impact 2018, which is awarded by Google, McKinsey and
Rocket Internet.